TEACHER'S PET PUBLICATIONS

PUZZLE PACK
for
The Good Earth

based on the book by
Pearl Buck

Written by
William T. Collins

© 2005 Teacher's Pet Publications
All Rights Reserved

The materials in this packet are copyrighted
by Teacher's Pet Publications, Inc.

These pages may be duplicated by the purchaser
for use in the purchaser's own classroom.

Copying any of these materials and distributing them
for any other purpose is a violation of the copyright laws.

© 2005 Teacher's Pet Publications, Inc.
www.tpet.com

INTRODUCTION
If you already own the LitPlan for this title, this Puzzle Pack will refresh your Unit Resource Materials and Vocabulary Resource Materials sections plus give you additional materials you can substitute into the tests. If you do not already have a complete LitPlan, these pages will give you some supplemental materials to use with your own plan. There are two main groups of materials: one set for unit words (such as characters' names, symbols, places, etc.) and one set for vocabulary words associated with the book.

WORD LIST
There is a word list for both the unit words and the vocabulary words. These lists show you which words are being used in the materials and the clues or definitions being used for those words. You may want to give students a word list with clues/definitions to help them, or you may want students to only have a word list (without clues/definitions) if you want them to work a little harder. Both are available for duplication. The word lists can also be your "calling key" for the bingo games.

FILL IN THE BLANK AND MATCHING
There are 4 each of the fill in the blank and matching worksheets for both the unit and vocabulary words. These pages can be used either as extra worksheets for students or as objective parts of a unit test. They can be done individually if students need extra help or as a whole class activity to review the material covered.

MAGIC SQUARES
The magic squares not only reinforce the material covered but also work on reasoning and math skills. Many teachers have told us that their students really enjoy doing these!

WORD SEARCH PUZZLES
The word search words go in all directions, as indicated on your answer keys. Two of the word search puzzles have the clues listed rather than the words. This makes the puzzle a little more difficult, but it reinforces the material better. Two word search puzzles have words only for students who find the clue puzzles too difficult.

CROSSWORD PUZZLES
Both unit and vocabulary word sections have 4 crossword puzzles.

BINGO CARDS
There are 32 individual bingo cards for the unit words and 32 individual bingo cards for the vocabulary words. You can use your word list as a "call list," calling the words at random and marking them off of your list as you go, or you could use the flash cards by cutting them apart and drawing the words at random from a hat (or box or whatever). To make a better review, you might ask for the definition and spelling of each word as you call it out–or you could call out the definitions and have students tell you the words they need to look for on the puzzle.

JUGGLE LETTERS
The vocabulary juggle letter game is intended to help students learn the spellings of the words. One sheet has the definitions listed on it as an extra help for students who need it or to reinforce the definitions if you choose to do so.

FLASH CARDS
We've included a set of vocabulary flash cards you can duplicate, cut, and fold for your students. Some teachers make a few sets for general use by the class; others make a set for each student. Some teachers duplicate them for each student and have the students cut & fold their own. You can cut out just the words and put them in a hat, have each student pick out one word and write the definition and a sentence for that word. Students then swap words and papers, with the next student adding a sentence of his own under the last one. You can have students swap as many times as you like. Each time the student will read the sentences written prior to his own and then add a sentence. You can cut out the words and definitions separately and play "I Have; Who Has?" Each student in the room draws a word and definition. The first student says, "I have (the name of the word). Who has the definition?" The student with the definition reads it then says, "I have (the name of the vocabulary word she has). Who has the definition?" The round continues until all words and definitions have been given.

Good Earth Word List

No.	Word	Clue/Definition
1.	BEG	WL's father would not do this.
2.	BLOSSOM	She promised to take care of Wang Lung's daughter.
3.	BRAID	WL cut off his ___.
4.	BUCK	Author
5.	CHINA	WL's country
6.	CHOKED	O-lan ___ the newborn child; it would have died of starvation.
7.	CUCKOO	Servant woman with whom WL bargained for land
8.	DEATH	WL claimed their child was a female with smallpox & prayed for its ___.
9.	EGGS	WL dyed these red and gave them to friends to celebrate the birth of his son.
10.	FEET	O-lan bound her daughter's ___.
11.	FLOOD	A great ___ came. (water disaster)
12.	FURNITURE	WL sold his ___ to get money to go south.
13.	HID	To escape soldiers, WL ___ during the day.
14.	HWANG	WL bought land from the House of ___.
15.	IDIOTS	Lotus called WL's children this.
16.	JEWELS	O-lan had ___ hidden in the cloth.
17.	LAND	Working on it made WL well again.
18.	LIFE	When WL cut off his braid, O-lan said, 'You have cut off your ___!'
19.	LOTUS	WL's first mistress
20.	LOVE	WL was ___-sick for Lotus.
21.	MEAT	WL would not eat the ___ his 2nd son stole.
22.	MONEY	WL gave his uncle ___ to protect his own reputation.
23.	NEPHEW	He went to join the war & see the country.
24.	OLAN	She married Wang Lung.
25.	OPIUM	WL gave his uncle's family this to make them less of a nuisance.
26.	OX	O-lan killed it for food.
27.	PROUD	Characteristic of Wang Lung; he was ___.
28.	RAT	'He lived in the rich city as alien as a ___ in a rich man's house.'
29.	ROBBERS	The uncle belonged to a band of ___.
30.	SCHOOL	WL sent his sons there to learn to read and write.
31.	SELLING	___ a female child was an accepted means of survival for the poor.
32.	SLAVE	O-lan's final words to Cuckoo: '...you are still a ___.'
33.	SOLD	The two sons ___ WL's land and divided the profits.
34.	SOLDIERS	They arrested poor men.
35.	SON	'When I return to that house it will be with my ___ in my arms.'
36.	SOUTH	Direction WL wanted to go to find food and work
37.	TRAIN	Transportation south
38.	UGLY	In the 7th year of prosperity, WL saw O-lan as ___.
39.	UNCLE	Wang Lung's ___'s family stayed in the house
40.	WANG	___ Lung had a strong attachment to the land.

Good Earth Fill In The Blanks 1

_____

_____

_____

_____

_____

_____

_____

_____

_____

_____

_____

_____

_____

_____

_____

_____

_____

_____

_____

_____

1. O-lan bound her daughter's ___.
2. WL claimed their child was a female with smallpox & prayed for its ___.
3. O-lan ___ the newborn child; it would have died of starvation.
4. WL was ___-sick for Lotus.
5. Transportation south
6. In the 7th year of prosperity, WL saw O-lan as ___.
7. ___ Lung had a strong attachment to the land.
8. Lotus called WL's children this.
9. WL dyed these red and gave them to friends to celebrate the birth of his son.
10. WL bought land from the House of ___.
11. 'He lived in the rich city as alien as a ___ in a rich man's house.'
12. O-lan's final words to Cuckoo: '...you are still a ___.'
13. To escape soldiers, WL ___ during the day.
14. WL would not eat the ___ his 2nd son stole.
15. 'When I return to that house it will be with my ___ in my arms.'
16. Characteristic of Wang Lung; he was ___.
17. O-lan had ___ hidden in the cloth.
18. WL's first mistress
19. WL gave his uncle ___ to protect his own reputation.
20. When WL cut off his braid, O-lan said, 'You have cut off your ___!'

Good Earth Fill In The Blanks 1 Answer Key

FEET	1. O-lan bound her daughter's ___.
DEATH	2. WL claimed their child was a female with smallpox & prayed for its ___.
CHOKED	3. O-lan ___ the newborn child; it would have died of starvation.
LOVE	4. WL was ___-sick for Lotus.
TRAIN	5. Transportation south
UGLY	6. In the 7th year of prosperity, WL saw O-lan as ___.
WANG	7. ___ Lung had a strong attachment to the land.
IDIOTS	8. Lotus called WL's children this.
EGGS	9. WL dyed these red and gave them to friends to celebrate the birth of his son.
HWANG	10. WL bought land from the House of ___.
RAT	11. 'He lived in the rich city as alien as a ___ in a rich man's house.'
SLAVE	12. O-lan's final words to Cuckoo: '...you are still a ___.'
HID	13. To escape soldiers, WL ___ during the day.
MEAT	14. WL would not eat the ___ his 2nd son stole.
SON	15. 'When I return to that house it will be with my ___ in my arms.'
PROUD	16. Characteristic of Wang Lung; he was ___.
JEWELS	17. O-lan had ___ hidden in the cloth.
LOTUS	18. WL's first mistress
MONEY	19. WL gave his uncle ___ to protect his own reputation.
LIFE	20. When WL cut off his braid, O-lan said, 'You have cut off your ___!'

Good Earth Fill In The Blanks 2

_____
_____
_____
_____
_____
_____
_____
_____
_____
_____
_____
_____
_____
_____
_____
_____
_____
_____
_____
_____

1. The two sons ___ WL's land and divided the profits.
2. Direction WL wanted to go to find food and work
3. They arrested poor men.
4. When WL cut off his braid, O-lan said, 'You have cut off your ___!'
5. 'When I return to that house it will be with my ___ in my arms.'
6. WL dyed these red and gave them to friends to celebrate the birth of his son.
7. ___ Lung had a strong attachment to the land.
8. O-lan killed it for food.
9. WL's country
10. A great ___ came. (water disaster)
11. WL gave his uncle's family this to make them less of a nuisance.
12. WL cut off his ___.
13. The uncle belonged to a band of ___.
14. Servant woman with whom WL bargained for land
15. ___ a female child was an accepted means of survival for the poor.
16. O-lan had ___ hidden in the cloth.
17. O-lan's final words to Cuckoo: '...you are still a ___.'
18. WL sent his sons there to learn to read and write.
19. She married Wang Lung.
20. WL claimed their child was a female with smallpox & prayed for its ___.

Good Earth Fill In The Blanks 2 Answer Key

SOLD	1. The two sons ___ WL's land and divided the profits.
SOUTH	2. Direction WL wanted to go to find food and work
SOLDIERS	3. They arrested poor men.
LIFE	4. When WL cut off his braid, O-lan said, 'You have cut off your ___!'
SON	5. 'When I return to that house it will be with my ___ in my arms.'
EGGS	6. WL dyed these red and gave them to friends to celebrate the birth of his son.
WANG	7. ___ Lung had a strong attachment to the land.
OX	8. O-lan killed it for food.
CHINA	9. WL's country
FLOOD	10. A great ___ came. (water disaster)
OPIUM	11. WL gave his uncle's family this to make them less of a nuisance.
BRAID	12. WL cut off his ___.
ROBBERS	13. The uncle belonged to a band of ___.
CUCKOO	14. Servant woman with whom WL bargained for land
SELLING	15. ___ a female child was an accepted means of survival for the poor.
JEWELS	16. O-lan had ___ hidden in the cloth.
SLAVE	17. O-lan's final words to Cuckoo: '...you are still a ___.'
SCHOOL	18. WL sent his sons there to learn to read and write.
OLAN	19. She married Wang Lung.
DEATH	20. WL claimed their child was a female with smallpox & prayed for its ___.

Good Earth Fill In The Blanks 3

_____ 1. WL's first mistress

_____ 2. Author

_____ 3. O-lan had ___ hidden in the cloth.

_____ 4. To escape soldiers, WL ___ during the day.

_____ 5. Lotus called WL's children this.

_____ 6. Direction WL wanted to go to find food and work

_____ 7. O-lan killed it for food.

_____ 8. O-lan bound her daughter's ___.

_____ 9. WL bought land from the House of ___.

_____ 10. When WL cut off his braid, O-lan said, 'You have cut off your ___!'

_____ 11. ___ Lung had a strong attachment to the land.

_____ 12. WL dyed these red and gave them to friends to celebrate the birth of his son.

                            13. Transportation south

_____ 14. WL cut off his ___.

                            15. In the 7th year of prosperity, WL saw O-lan as ___.

_____ 16. A great ___ came. (water disaster)

                            17. WL gave his uncle's family this to make them less of a nuisance.

_____ 18. WL sent his sons there to learn to read and write.

                            19. WL would not eat the ___ his 2nd son stole.

_____ 20. WL was ___-sick for Lotus.

9
Copyrighted

Good Earth Fill In The Blanks 3 Answer Key

LOTUS	1. WL's first mistress
BUCK	2. Author
JEWELS	3. O-lan had ___ hidden in the cloth.
HID	4. To escape soldiers, WL ___ during the day.
IDIOTS	5. Lotus called WL's children this.
SOUTH	6. Direction WL wanted to go to find food and work
OX	7. O-lan killed it for food.
FEET	8. O-lan bound her daughter's ___.
HWANG	9. WL bought land from the House of ___.
LIFE	10. When WL cut off his braid, O-lan said, 'You have cut off your ___!'
WANG	11. ___ Lung had a strong attachment to the land.
EGGS	12. WL dyed these red and gave them to friends to celebrate the birth of his son.
TRAIN	13. Transportation south
BRAID	14. WL cut off his ___.
UGLY	15. In the 7th year of prosperity, WL saw O-lan as ___.
FLOOD	16. A great ___ came. (water disaster)
OPIUM	17. WL gave his uncle's family this to make them less of a nuisance.
SCHOOL	18. WL sent his sons there to learn to read and write.
MEAT	19. WL would not eat the ___ his 2nd son stole.
LOVE	20. WL was ___-sick for Lotus.

Good Earth Fill In The Blanks 4

_____
_____
_____
_____
_____
_____
_____
_____
_____
_____
_____
_____
_____
_____
_____
_____
_____
_____
_____
_____

1. The two sons ___ WL's land and divided the profits.
2. WL bought land from the House of ___.
3. WL cut off his ___.
4. To escape soldiers, WL ___ during the day.
5. O-lan's final words to Cuckoo: '...you are still a ___.'
6. O-lan had ___ hidden in the cloth.
7. The uncle belonged to a band of ___.
8. 'He lived in the rich city as alien as a ___ in a rich man's house.'
9. WL gave his uncle ___ to protect his own reputation.
10. She married Wang Lung.
11. Lotus called WL's children this.
12. WL sold his ___ to get money to go south.
13. WL was ___-sick for Lotus.
14. They arrested poor men.
15. He went to join the war & see the country.
16. In the 7th year of prosperity, WL saw O-lan as ___.
17. Direction WL wanted to go to find food and work
18. Transportation south
19. WL sent his sons there to learn to read and write.
20. WL gave his uncle's family this to make them less of a nuisance.

Good Earth Fill In The Blanks 4 Answer Key

SOLD	1. The two sons ___ WL's land and divided the profits.
HWANG	2. WL bought land from the House of ___.
BRAID	3. WL cut off his ___.
HID	4. To escape soldiers, WL ___ during the day.
SLAVE	5. O-lan's final words to Cuckoo: '...you are still a ___.'
JEWELS	6. O-lan had ___ hidden in the cloth.
ROBBERS	7. The uncle belonged to a band of ___.
RAT	8. 'He lived in the rich city as alien as a ___ in a rich man's house.'
MONEY	9. WL gave his uncle ___ to protect his own reputation.
OLAN	10. She married Wang Lung.
IDIOTS	11. Lotus called WL's children this.
FURNITURE	12. WL sold his ___ to get money to go south.
LOVE	13. WL was ___-sick for Lotus.
SOLDIERS	14. They arrested poor men.
NEPHEW	15. He went to join the war & see the country.
UGLY	16. In the 7th year of prosperity, WL saw O-lan as ___.
SOUTH	17. Direction WL wanted to go to find food and work
TRAIN	18. Transportation south
SCHOOL	19. WL sent his sons there to learn to read and write.
OPIUM	20. WL gave his uncle's family this to make them less of a nuisance.

Good Earth Matching 1

___ 1. NEPHEW   A. WL bought land from the House of ___.
___ 2. HID   B. O-lan killed it for food.
___ 3. FLOOD   C. To escape soldiers, WL ___ during the day.
___ 4. SLAVE   D. A great ___ came. (water disaster)
___ 5. OPIUM   E. The uncle belonged to a band of ___.
___ 6. FEET   F. Servant woman with whom WL bargained for land
___ 7. BEG   G. WL's first mistress
___ 8. FURNITURE   H. Lotus called WL's children this.
___ 9. ROBBERS   I. WL dyed these red and gave them to friends to celebrate the birth of his son.
___ 10. LOTUS   J. ___ a female child was an accepted means of survival for the poor.
___ 11. EGGS   K. O-lan ___ the newborn child; it would have died of starvation.
___ 12. LAND   L. WL cut off his ___.
___ 13. HWANG   M. WL claimed their child was a female with smallpox & prayed for its ___.
___ 14. BRAID   N. WL gave his uncle's family this to make them less of a nuisance.
___ 15. SOUTH   O. Direction WL wanted to go to find food and work
___ 16. CHOKED   P. WL was ___-sick for Lotus.
___ 17. OX   Q. WL sent his sons there to learn to read and write.
___ 18. LOVE   R. O-lan's final words to Cuckoo: '...you are still a ___.'
___ 19. DEATH   S. 'He lived in the rich city as alien as a ___ in a rich man's house.'
___ 20. TRAIN   T. He went to join the war & see the country.
___ 21. SCHOOL   U. O-lan bound her daughter's ___.
___ 22. RAT   V. WL sold his ___ to get money to go south.
___ 23. CUCKOO   W. WL's father would not do this.
___ 24. SELLING   X. Working on it made WL well again.
___ 25. IDIOTS   Y. Transportation south

Good Earth Matching 1 Answer Key

T - 1. NEPHEW A. WL bought land from the House of ___.
C - 2. HID B. O-lan killed it for food.
D - 3. FLOOD C. To escape soldiers, WL ___ during the day.
R - 4. SLAVE D. A great ___ came. (water disaster)
N - 5. OPIUM E. The uncle belonged to a band of ___.
U - 6. FEET F. Servant woman with whom WL bargained for land
W - 7. BEG G. WL's first mistress
V - 8. FURNITURE H. Lotus called WL's children this.
E - 9. ROBBERS I. WL dyed these red and gave them to friends to celebrate the birth of his son.
G - 10. LOTUS J. ___ a female child was an accepted means of survival for the poor.
I - 11. EGGS K. O-lan ___ the newborn child; it would have died of starvation.
X - 12. LAND L. WL cut off his ___.
A - 13. HWANG M. WL claimed their child was a female with smallpox & prayed for its ___.
L - 14. BRAID N. WL gave his uncle's family this to make them less of a nuisance.
O - 15. SOUTH O. Direction WL wanted to go to find food and work
K - 16. CHOKED P. WL was ___-sick for Lotus.
B - 17. OX Q. WL sent his sons there to learn to read and write.
P - 18. LOVE R. O-lan's final words to Cuckoo: '...you are still a ___.'
M - 19. DEATH S. 'He lived in the rich city as alien as a ___ in a rich man's house.'
Y - 20. TRAIN T. He went to join the war & see the country.
Q - 21. SCHOOL U. O-lan bound her daughter's ___.
S - 22. RAT V. WL sold his ___ to get money to go south.
F - 23. CUCKOO W. WL's father would not do this.
J - 24. SELLING X. Working on it made WL well again.
H - 25. IDIOTS Y. Transportation south

Good Earth Matching 2

___ 1. TRAIN
___ 2. WANG
___ 3. ROBBERS
___ 4. OPIUM
___ 5. RAT
___ 6. MONEY
___ 7. OX
___ 8. BUCK
___ 9. LIFE
___ 10. SLAVE
___ 11. JEWELS
___ 12. CHINA
___ 13. SOLDIERS
___ 14. FURNITURE
___ 15. FEET
___ 16. FLOOD
___ 17. NEPHEW
___ 18. DEATH
___ 19. OLAN
___ 20. SELLING
___ 21. BLOSSOM
___ 22. BEG
___ 23. LAND
___ 24. CUCKOO
___ 25. SOUTH

A. WL's father would not do this.
B. Direction WL wanted to go to find food and work
C. Author
D. ___ Lung had a strong attachment to the land.
E. Servant woman with whom WL bargained for land
F. WL's country
G. O-lan's final words to Cuckoo: '...you are still a ___.'
H. She married Wang Lung.
I. She promised to take care of Wang Lung's daughter.
J. ___ a female child was an accepted means of survival for the poor.
K. O-lan bound her daughter's ___.
L. O-lan had ___ hidden in the cloth.
M. When WL cut off his braid, O-lan said, 'You have cut off your ___!'
N. WL claimed their child was a female with smallpox & prayed for its ___.
O. Working on it made WL well again.
P. He went to join the war & see the country.
Q. Transportation south
R. WL gave his uncle's family this to make them less of a nuisance.
S. O-lan killed it for food.
T. They arrested poor men.
U. 'He lived in the rich city as alien as a ___ in a rich man's house.'
V. A great ___ came. (water disaster)
W. WL gave his uncle ___ to protect his own reputation.
X. The uncle belonged to a band of ___.
Y. WL sold his ___ to get money to go south.

Good Earth Matching 2 Answer Key

Q - 1. TRAIN   A. WL's father would not do this.
D - 2. WANG   B. Direction WL wanted to go to find food and work
X - 3. ROBBERS   C. Author
R - 4. OPIUM   D. ___ Lung had a strong attachment to the land.
U - 5. RAT   E. Servant woman with whom WL bargained for land
W - 6. MONEY   F. WL's country
S - 7. OX   G. O-lan's final words to Cuckoo: '...you are still a ___.'
C - 8. BUCK   H. She married Wang Lung.
M - 9. LIFE   I. She promised to take care of Wang Lung's daughter.
G - 10. SLAVE   J. ___ a female child was an accepted means of survival for the poor.
L - 11. JEWELS   K. O-lan bound her daughter's ___.
F - 12. CHINA   L. O-lan had ___ hidden in the cloth.
T - 13. SOLDIERS   M. When WL cut off his braid, O-lan said, 'You have cut off your ___!'
Y - 14. FURNITURE   N. WL claimed their child was a female with smallpox & prayed for its ___.
K - 15. FEET   O. Working on it made WL well again.
V - 16. FLOOD   P. He went to join the war & see the country.
P - 17. NEPHEW   Q. Transportation south
N - 18. DEATH   R. WL gave his uncle's family this to make them less of a nuisance.
H - 19. OLAN   S. O-lan killed it for food.
J - 20. SELLING   T. They arrested poor men.
I - 21. BLOSSOM   U. 'He lived in the rich city as alien as a ___ in a rich man's house.'
A - 22. BEG   V. A great ___ came. (water disaster)
O - 23. LAND   W. WL gave his uncle ___ to protect his own reputation.
E - 24. CUCKOO   X. The uncle belonged to a band of ___.
B - 25. SOUTH   Y. WL sold his ___ to get money to go south.

Good Earth Matching 3

___ 1. IDIOTS   A. WL sent his sons there to learn to read and write.
___ 2. JEWELS   B. O-lan killed it for food.
___ 3. RAT   C. Lotus called WL's children this.
___ 4. CUCKOO   D. O-lan ___ the newborn child; it would have died of starvation.
___ 5. SOLDIERS   E. ___ Lung had a strong attachment to the land.
___ 6. LIFE   F. She married Wang Lung.
___ 7. UGLY   G. O-lan bound her daughter's ___.
___ 8. BUCK   H. WL was ___-sick for Lotus.
___ 9. HID   I. WL sold his ___ to get money to go south.
___10. FEET   J. O-lan had ___ hidden in the cloth.
___11. SOLD   K. 'He lived in the rich city as alien as a ___ in a rich man's house.'
___12. OLAN   L. To escape soldiers, WL ___ during the day.
___13. UNCLE   M. In the 7th year of prosperity, WL saw O-lan as ___.
___14. SOUTH   N. Direction WL wanted to go to find food and work
___15. LAND   O. Servant woman with whom WL bargained for land
___16. SON   P. The two sons ___ WL's land and divided the profits.
___17. SELLING   Q. She promised to take care of Wang Lung's daughter.
___18. OX   R. ___ a female child was an accepted means of survival for the poor.
___19. CHOKED   S. Author
___20. LOVE   T. Working on it made WL well again.
___21. SCHOOL   U. They arrested poor men.
___22. WANG   V. 'When I return to that house it will be with my ___ in my arms.'
___23. BLOSSOM   W. WL would not eat the ___ his 2nd son stole.
___24. MEAT   X. When WL cut off his braid, O-lan said, 'You have cut off your ___!'
___25. FURNITURE Y. Wang Lung's ___'s family stayed in the house

Good Earth Matching 3 Answer Key

C - 1. IDIOTS
J - 2. JEWELS
K - 3. RAT
O - 4. CUCKOO
U - 5. SOLDIERS
X - 6. LIFE
M - 7. UGLY
S - 8. BUCK
L - 9. HID
G - 10. FEET
P - 11. SOLD
F - 12. OLAN
Y - 13. UNCLE
N - 14. SOUTH
T - 15. LAND
V - 16. SON
R - 17. SELLING
B - 18. OX
D - 19. CHOKED
H - 20. LOVE
A - 21. SCHOOL
E - 22. WANG
Q - 23. BLOSSOM
W - 24. MEAT
I - 25. FURNITURE

A. WL sent his sons there to learn to read and write.
B. O-lan killed it for food.
C. Lotus called WL's children this.
D. O-lan ___ the newborn child; it would have died of starvation.
E. ___ Lung had a strong attachment to the land.
F. She married Wang Lung.
G. O-lan bound her daughter's ___.
H. WL was ___-sick for Lotus.
I. WL sold his ___ to get money to go south.
J. O-lan had ___ hidden in the cloth.
K. 'He lived in the rich city as alien as a ___ in a rich man's house.'
L. To escape soldiers, WL ___ during the day.
M. In the 7th year of prosperity, WL saw O-lan as ___.
N. Direction WL wanted to go to find food and work
O. Servant woman with whom WL bargained for land
P. The two sons ___ WL's land and divided the profits.
Q. She promised to take care of Wang Lung's daughter.
R. ___ a female child was an accepted means of survival for the poor.
S. Author
T. Working on it made WL well again.
U. They arrested poor men.
V. 'When I return to that house it will be with my ___ in my arms.'
W. WL would not eat the ___ his 2nd son stole.
X. When WL cut off his braid, O-lan said, 'You have cut off your ___!'
Y. Wang Lung's ___'s family stayed in the house

Good Earth Matching 4

___ 1. BLOSSOM
___ 2. LOVE
___ 3. PROUD
___ 4. FURNITURE
___ 5. SELLING
___ 6. SCHOOL
___ 7. MEAT
___ 8. HID
___ 9. BRAID
___10. UNCLE
___11. SOLD
___12. WANG
___13. UGLY
___14. SOLDIERS
___15. SLAVE
___16. BUCK
___17. NEPHEW
___18. ROBBERS
___19. SOUTH
___20. CUCKOO
___21. EGGS
___22. SON
___23. CHOKED
___24. CHINA
___25. FLOOD

A. In the 7th year of prosperity, WL saw O-lan as ___.
B. ___ a female child was an accepted means of survival for the poor.
C. To escape soldiers, WL ___ during the day.
D. 'When I return to that house it will be with my ___ in my arms.'
E. WL sold his ___ to get money to go south.
F. ___ Lung had a strong attachment to the land.
G. Author
H. WL dyed these red and gave them to friends to celebrate the birth of his son.
I. A great ___ came. (water disaster)
J. O-lan ___ the newborn child; it would have died of starvation.
K. They arrested poor men.
L. O-lan's final words to Cuckoo: '...you are still a ___.'
M. She promised to take care of Wang Lung's daughter.
N. The two sons ___ WL's land and divided the profits.
O. WL cut off his ___.
P. WL was ___-sick for Lotus.
Q. WL sent his sons there to learn to read and write.
R. Direction WL wanted to go to find food and work
S. The uncle belonged to a band of ___.
T. Characteristic of Wang Lung; he was ___.
U. WL would not eat the ___ his 2nd son stole.
V. WL's country
W. Wang Lung's ___'s family stayed in the house
X. He went to join the war & see the country.
Y. Servant woman with whom WL bargained for land

Good Earth Matching 4 Answer Key

M - 1.	BLOSSOM	A. In the 7th year of prosperity, WL saw O-lan as ___.
P - 2.	LOVE	B. ___ a female child was an accepted means of survival for the poor.
T - 3.	PROUD	C. To escape soldiers, WL ___ during the day.
E - 4.	FURNITURE	D. 'When I return to that house it will be with my ___ in my arms.'
B - 5.	SELLING	E. WL sold his ___ to get money to go south.
Q - 6.	SCHOOL	F. ___ Lung had a strong attachment to the land.
U - 7.	MEAT	G. Author
C - 8.	HID	H. WL dyed these red and gave them to friends to celebrate the birth of his son.
O - 9.	BRAID	I. A great ___ came. (water disaster)
W - 10.	UNCLE	J. O-lan ___ the newborn child; it would have died of starvation.
N - 11.	SOLD	K. They arrested poor men.
F - 12.	WANG	L. O-lan's final words to Cuckoo: '...you are still a ___.'
A - 13.	UGLY	M. She promised to take care of Wang Lung's daughter.
K - 14.	SOLDIERS	N. The two sons ___ WL's land and divided the profits.
L - 15.	SLAVE	O. WL cut off his ___.
G - 16.	BUCK	P. WL was ___-sick for Lotus.
X - 17.	NEPHEW	Q. WL sent his sons there to learn to read and write.
S - 18.	ROBBERS	R. Direction WL wanted to go to find food and work
R - 19.	SOUTH	S. The uncle belonged to a band of ___.
Y - 20.	CUCKOO	T. Characteristic of Wang Lung; he was ___.
H - 21.	EGGS	U. WL would not eat the ___ his 2nd son stole.
D - 22.	SON	V. WL's country
J - 23.	CHOKED	W. Wang Lung's ___'s family stayed in the house
V - 24.	CHINA	X. He went to join the war & see the country.
I - 25.	FLOOD	Y. Servant woman with whom WL bargained for land

Good Earth Magic Squares 1

Match the definition with the vocabulary word. Put your answers in the magic squares below. When your answers are correct, all columns and rows will add to the same number.

A. SCHOOL   E. PROUD   I. CUCKOO   M. UGLY
B. FLOOD   F. HID   J. DEATH   N. SOUTH
C. RAT   G. BEG   K. UNCLE   O. BUCK
D. FURNITURE   H. CHINA   L. SOLD   P. LOVE

1. A great ___ came. (water disaster)
2. WL's father would not do this.
3. Wang Lung's ___'s family stayed in the house
4. Direction WL wanted to go to find food and work
5. In the 7th year of prosperity, WL saw O-lan as ___.
6. The two sons ___ WL's land and divided the profits.
7. WL's country
8. WL sent his sons there to learn to read and write.
9. WL was ___-sick for Lotus.
10. Servant woman with whom WL bargained for land
11. Characteristic of Wang Lung; he was ___.
12. WL sold his ___ to get money to go south.
13. 'He lived in the rich city as alien as a ___ in a rich man's house.'
14. To escape soldiers, WL ___ during the day.
15. WL claimed their child was a female with smallpox & prayed for its ___.
16. Author

A=	B=	C=	D=
E=	F=	G=	H=
I=	J=	K=	L=
M=	N=	O=	P=

Good Earth Magic Squares 1 Answer Key

Match the definition with the vocabulary word. Put your answers in the magic squares below. When your answers are correct, all columns and rows will add to the same number.

A. SCHOOL   E. PROUD   I. CUCKOO   M. UGLY
B. FLOOD   F. HID   J. DEATH   N. SOUTH
C. RAT   G. BEG   K. UNCLE   O. BUCK
D. FURNITURE   H. CHINA   L. SOLD   P. LOVE

1. A great ___ came. (water disaster)
2. WL's father would not do this.
3. Wang Lung's ___'s family stayed in the house
4. Direction WL wanted to go to find food and work
5. In the 7th year of prosperity, WL saw O-lan as ___.
6. The two sons ___ WL's land and divided the profits.
7. WL's country
8. WL sent his sons there to learn to read and write.
9. WL was ___-sick for Lotus.
10. Servant woman with whom WL bargained for land
11. Characteristic of Wang Lung; he was ___.
12. WL sold his ___ to get money to go south.
13. 'He lived in the rich city as alien as a ___ in a rich man's house.'
14. To escape soldiers, WL ___ during the day.
15. WL claimed their child was a female with smallpox & prayed for its ___.
16. Author

A=8	B=1	C=13	D=12
E=11	F=14	G=2	H=7
I=10	J=15	K=3	L=6
M=5	N=4	O=16	P=9

Good Earth Magic Squares 2

Match the definition with the vocabulary word. Put your answers in the magic squares below. When your answers are correct, all columns and rows will add to the same number.

A. SOLD
B. MONEY
C. SOUTH
D. IDIOTS
E. SLAVE
F. LOTUS
G. NEPHEW
H. HWANG
I. BLOSSOM
J. CHINA
K. LAND
L. UGLY
M. BRAID
N. RAT
O. SOLDIERS
P. PROUD

1. WL bought land from the House of ___.
2. The two sons ___ WL's land and divided the profits.
3. WL gave his uncle ___ to protect his own reputation.
4. He went to join the war & see the country.
5. WL's country
6. They arrested poor men.
7. Characteristic of Wang Lung; he was ___.
8. She promised to take care of Wang Lung's daughter.
9. Working on it made WL well again.
10. 'He lived in the rich city as alien as a ___ in a rich man's house.'
11. WL cut off his ___.
12. In the 7th year of prosperity, WL saw O-lan as ___.
13. O-lan's final words to Cuckoo: '...you are still a ___.'
14. Lotus called WL's children this.
15. Direction WL wanted to go to find food and work
16. WL's first mistress

A=	B=	C=	D=
E=	F=	G=	H=
I=	J=	K=	L=
M=	N=	O=	P=

Good Earth Magic Squares 2 Answer Key

Match the definition with the vocabulary word. Put your answers in the magic squares below. When your answers are correct, all columns and rows will add to the same number.

A. SOLD
B. MONEY
C. SOUTH
D. IDIOTS
E. SLAVE
F. LOTUS
G. NEPHEW
H. HWANG
I. BLOSSOM
J. CHINA
K. LAND
L. UGLY
M. BRAID
N. RAT
O. SOLDIERS
P. PROUD

1. WL bought land from the House of ___.
2. The two sons ___ WL's land and divided the profits.
3. WL gave his uncle ___ to protect his own reputation.
4. He went to join the war & see the country.
5. WL's country
6. They arrested poor men.
7. Characteristic of Wang Lung; he was ___.
8. She promised to take care of Wang Lung's daughter.
9. Working on it made WL well again.
10. 'He lived in the rich city as alien as a ___ in a rich man's house.'
11. WL cut off his ___.
12. In the 7th year of prosperity, WL saw O-lan as ___.
13. O-lan's final words to Cuckoo: '...you are still a ___.'
14. Lotus called WL's children this.
15. Direction WL wanted to go to find food and work
16. WL's first mistress

A=2	B=3	C=15	D=14
E=13	F=16	G=4	H=1
I=8	J=5	K=9	L=12
M=11	N=10	O=6	P=7

Good Earth Magic Squares 3

Match the definition with the vocabulary word. Put your answers in the magic squares below. When your answers are correct, all columns and rows will add to the same number.

A. LOVE   E. FURNITURE   I. WANG   M. BLOSSOM
B. OX   F. CUCKOO   J. SOLD   N. SLAVE
C. FLOOD   G. MEAT   K. FEET   O. LIFE
D. UNCLE   H. BEG   L. IDIOTS   P. TRAIN

1. A great ___ came. (water disaster)
2. The two sons ___ WL's land and divided the profits.
3. Servant woman with whom WL bargained for land
4. When WL cut off his braid, O-lan said, 'You have cut off your ___!'
5. Transportation south
6. WL sold his ___ to get money to go south.
7. ___ Lung had a strong attachment to the land.
8. Wang Lung's ___'s family stayed in the house
9. She promised to take care of Wang Lung's daughter.
10. WL's father would not do this.
11. Lotus called WL's children this.
12. WL was ___-sick for Lotus.
13. O-lan killed it for food.
14. O-lan bound her daughter's ___.
15. WL would not eat the ___ his 2nd son stole.
16. O-lan's final words to Cuckoo: '...you are still a ___.'

A=	B=	C=	D=
E=	F=	G=	H=
I=	J=	K=	L=
M=	N=	O=	P=

Good Earth Magic Squares 3 Answer Key

Match the definition with the vocabulary word. Put your answers in the magic squares below. When your answers are correct, all columns and rows will add to the same number.

A. LOVE
B. OX
C. FLOOD
D. UNCLE
E. FURNITURE
F. CUCKOO
G. MEAT
H. BEG
I. WANG
J. SOLD
K. FEET
L. IDIOTS
M. BLOSSOM
N. SLAVE
O. LIFE
P. TRAIN

1. A great ___ came. (water disaster)
2. The two sons ___ WL's land and divided the profits.
3. Servant woman with whom WL bargained for land
4. When WL cut off his braid, O-lan said, 'You have cut off your ___!'
5. Transportation south
6. WL sold his ___ to get money to go south.
7. ___ Lung had a strong attachment to the land.
8. Wang Lung's ___'s family stayed in the house
9. She promised to take care of Wang Lung's daughter.
10. WL's father would not do this.
11. Lotus called WL's children this.
12. WL was ___-sick for Lotus.
13. O-lan killed it for food.
14. O-lan bound her daughter's ___.
15. WL would not eat the ___ his 2nd son stole.
16. O-lan's final words to Cuckoo: '...you are still a ___.'

A=12	B=13	C=1	D=8
E=6	F=3	G=15	H=10
I=7	J=2	K=14	L=11
M=9	N=16	O=4	P=5

Good Earth Magic Squares 4

Match the definition with the vocabulary word. Put your answers in the magic squares below. When your answers are correct, all columns and rows will add to the same number.

A. WANG   E. OX   I. FEET   M. SOLD
B. DEATH   F. LAND   J. BLOSSOM   N. MONEY
C. FLOOD   G. HID   K. BEG   O. BRAID
D. ROBBERS   H. MEAT   L. FURNITURE P. IDIOTS

1. WL cut off his ___.
2. She promised to take care of Wang Lung's daughter.
3. WL would not eat the ___ his 2nd son stole.
4. ___ Lung had a strong attachment to the land.
5. The uncle belonged to a band of ___.
6. O-lan killed it for food.
7. WL's father would not do this.
8. WL gave his uncle ___ to protect his own reputation.
9. Working on it made WL well again.
10. A great ___ came. (water disaster)
11. The two sons ___ WL's land and divided the profits.
12. WL sold his ___ to get money to go south.
13. O-lan bound her daughter's ___.
14. Lotus called WL's children this.
15. WL claimed their child was a female with smallpox & prayed for its ___.
16. To escape soldiers, WL ___ during the day.

A=	B=	C=	D=
E=	F=	G=	H=
I=	J=	K=	L=
M=	N=	O=	P=

Good Earth Magic Squares 4 Answer Key

Match the definition with the vocabulary word. Put your answers in the magic squares below. When your answers are correct, all columns and rows will add to the same number.

A. WANG   E. OX   I. FEET   M. SOLD
B. DEATH   F. LAND   J. BLOSSOM   N. MONEY
C. FLOOD   G. HID   K. BEG   O. BRAID
D. ROBBERS   H. MEAT   L. FURNITURE   P. IDIOTS

1. WL cut off his ___.
2. She promised to take care of Wang Lung's daughter.
3. WL would not eat the ___ his 2nd son stole.
4. ___ Lung had a strong attachment to the land.
5. The uncle belonged to a band of ___.
6. O-lan killed it for food.
7. WL's father would not do this.
8. WL gave his uncle ___ to protect his own reputation.
9. Working on it made WL well again.
10. A great ___ came. (water disaster)
11. The two sons ___ WL's land and divided the profits.
12. WL sold his ___ to get money to go south.
13. O-lan bound her daughter's ___.
14. Lotus called WL's children this.
15. WL claimed their child was a female with smallpox & prayed for its ___.
16. To escape soldiers, WL ___ during the day.

A=4	B=15	C=10	D=5
E=6	F=9	G=16	H=3
I=13	J=2	K=7	L=12
M=11	N=8	O=1	P=14

Good Earth Word Search 1

Words are placed backwards, forward, diagonally, up and down. Clues listed below can help you find the words. Circle the hidden vocabulary words in the maze.

```
S C L D B Q B N H H R K U R R Q K
D E K O H C E B T O L A N S L A V E
J V C O V S G A U R L M C T V S U S
R R U L C E E X O X A Y L O M C G G
L J B F W M C Z S V S I E I L G L J
X O X L O O H C S F L S N D E A Y Q
Q B T P X T I I C U E M O I F E N H
G Q I U A N N B D R W E S L N C W D
S U C E S E A L H N E M T O D U A N
M O D L E P G O W I J X M S U C N Y
S P L Q L H T S A T D P N N O K G L
R A T D L E M S N U L I F E R O R H
E N F L I W J O G R K P B D P O Y V
B W T S N E G M P E C V Y M G J X J
B C S L G B R A I D T Q T L J Z C D
O P L D H L R S N B S G M M C F P N
R P S N L L V B H Y D Z L C R F C S
```

'He lived in the rich city as alien as a ___ in a rich man's house.' (3)
'When I return to that house it will be with my ___ in my arms.' (3)
A great ___ came. (water disaster) (5)
Author (4)
Characteristic of Wang Lung; he was ___. (5)
Direction WL wanted to go to find food and work (5)
He went to join the war & see the country. (6)
In the 7th year of prosperity, WL saw O-lan as ___. (4)
Lotus called WL's children this. (6)
O-lan ___ the newborn child; it would have died of starvation. (6)
O-lan bound her daughter's ___. (4)
O-lan had ___ hidden in the cloth. (6)
O-lan killed it for food. (2)
O-lan's final words to Cuckoo: '...you are still a ___.' (5)
Servant woman with whom WL bargained for land (6)
She married Wang Lung. (4)
She promised to take care of Wang Lung's daughter. (7)
The two sons ___ WL's land and divided the profits. (4)
The uncle belonged to a band of ___. (7)
They arrested poor men. (8)
To escape soldiers, WL ___ during the day. (3)
Transportation south (5)
WL bought land from the House of ___. (5)
WL claimed their child was a female with smallpox & prayed for its ___. (5)
WL cut off his __. (5)
WL dyed these red and gave them to friends to celebrate the birth of his son. (4)
WL gave his uncle ___ to protect his own reputation. (5)
WL gave his uncle's family this to make them less of a nuisance. (5)
WL sent his sons there to learn to read and write. (6)
WL sold his ___ to get money to go south. (9)
WL was ___-sick for Lotus. (4)
WL would not eat the ___ his 2nd son stole. (4)
WL's country (5)
WL's father would not do this. (3)
WL's first mistress (5)
Wang Lung's ___'s family stayed in the house (5)
When WL cut off his braid, O-lan said, 'You have cut off your ___!' (4)
Working on it made WL well again. (4)
___ Lung had a strong attachment to the land. (4)
___ a female child was an accepted means of survival for the poor. (7)

Good Earth Word Search 1 Answer Key

Words are placed backwards, forward, diagonally, up and down. Clues listed below can help you find the words. Circle the hidden vocabulary words in the maze.

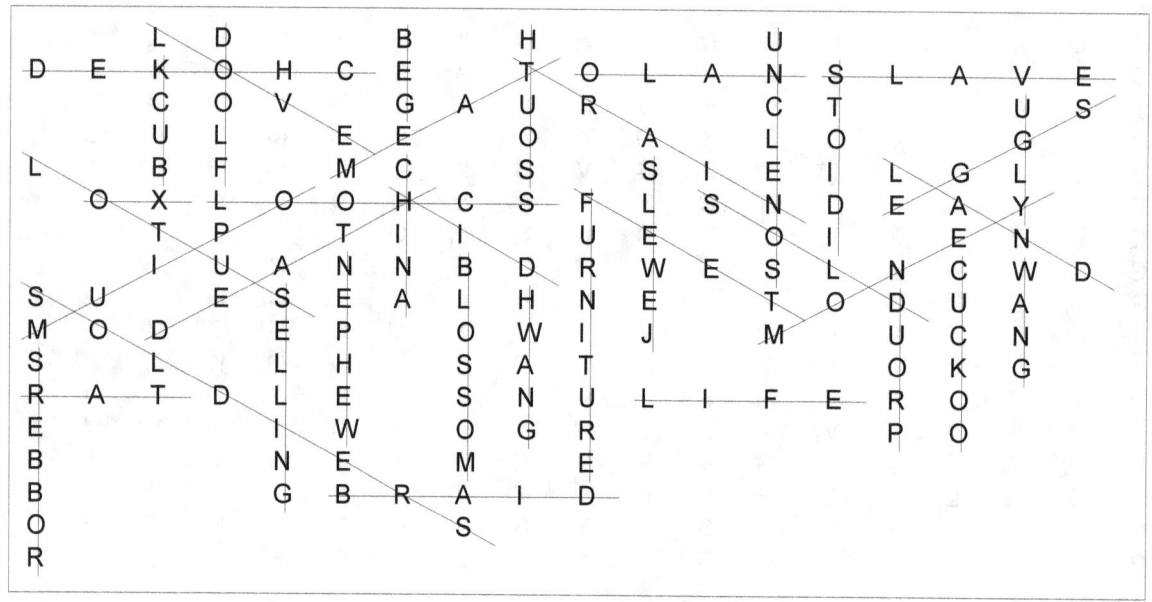

'He lived in the rich city as alien as a ___ in a rich man's house.' (3)

'When I return to that house it will be with my ___ in my arms.' (3)

A great ___ came. (water disaster) (5)

Author (4)

Characteristic of Wang Lung; he was ___. (5)

Direction WL wanted to go to find food and work (5)

He went to join the war & see the country. (6)

In the 7th year of prosperity, WL saw O-lan as ___. (4)

Lotus called WL's children this. (6)

O-lan ___ the newborn child; it would have died of starvation. (6)

O-lan bound her daughter's ___. (4)

O-lan had ___ hidden in the cloth. (6)

O-lan killed it for food. (2)

O-lan's final words to Cuckoo: '...you are still a ___.' (5)

Servant woman with whom WL bargained for land (6)

She married Wang Lung. (4)

She promised to take care of Wang Lung's daughter. (7)

The two sons ___ WL's land and divided the profits. (4)

The uncle belonged to a band of ___. (7)

They arrested poor men. (8)

To escape soldiers, WL ___ during the day. (3)

Transportation south (5)

WL bought land from the House of ___. (5)

WL claimed their child was a female with smallpox & prayed for its ___. (5)

WL cut off his ___. (5)

WL dyed these red and gave them to friends to celebrate the birth of his son. (4)

WL gave his uncle ___ to protect his own reputation. (5)

WL gave his uncle's family this to make them less of a nuisance. (5)

WL sent his sons there to learn to read and write. (6)

WL sold his ___ to get money to go south. (9)

WL was ___-sick for Lotus. (4)

WL would not eat the ___ his 2nd son stole. (4)

WL's country (5)

WL's father would not do this. (3)

WL's first mistress (5)

Wang Lung's ___'s family stayed in the house (5)

When WL cut off his braid, O-lan said, 'You have cut off your ___!' (4)

Working on it made WL well again. (4)

___ Lung had a strong attachment to the land. (4)

___ a female child was an accepted means of survival for the poor. (7)

Good Earth Word Search 2

Words are placed backwards, forward, diagonally, up and down. Clues listed below can help you find the words. Circle the hidden vocabulary words in the maze.

```
F S O L D I E R S R P X Y I D C S V
L L B A V J E C T V A E V D M U O H
O A R N R V H R A H N T P I T Z L L
O V A D O O C D E O X G D O R R D W
D E I L O E H K M H D N L T X S O X
K P D L L J I D R U O A Y S L J S V
R T H C Q S N C O S R W N E B Z C Q
C O N D Y D A R Z N S M W T L Y T S
B U B C K B P H I D K E C U C K O O
L U M B H R S T F R J V W T Q D G X
G P C C E O Z K Y W M N W X L L H P
Q D P K H R K H K O O E K C F R W K
T R A I N E S E S D W P J B Y L G U
B S G P X F F S D E O H I D W N G S
Y E K N M I O X F A L E T U A M H N
D V G N I L L E S T A W N W M H S Q
E G G S B F E E T H N G H T U O S H
```

'He lived in the rich city as alien as a ___ in a rich man's house.' (3)
'When I return to that house it will be with my ___ in my arms.' (3)
A great ___ came. (water disaster) (5)
Author (4)
Characteristic of Wang Lung; he was ___. (5)
Direction WL wanted to go to find food and work (5)
He went to join the war & see the country. (6)
In the 7th year of prosperity, WL saw O-lan as ___. (4)
Lotus called WL's children this. (6)
O-lan ___ the newborn child; it would have died of starvation. (6)
O-lan bound her daughter's ___. (4)
O-lan had ___ hidden in the cloth. (6)
O-lan killed it for food. (2)
O-lan's final words to Cuckoo: '...you are still a ___.' (5)
Servant woman with whom WL bargained for land (6)
She married Wang Lung. (4)
She promised to take care of Wang Lung's daughter. (7)
The two sons ___ WL's land and divided the profits. (4)
The uncle belonged to a band of ___. (7)

They arrested poor men. (8)
To escape soldiers, WL ___ during the day. (3)
Transportation south (5)
WL bought land from the House of ___. (5)
WL claimed their child was a female with smallpox & prayed for its ___. (5)
WL cut off his __. (5)
WL dyed these red and gave them to friends to celebrate the birth of his son. (4)
WL gave his uncle ___ to protect his own reputation. (5)
WL gave his uncle's family this to make them less of a nuisance. (5)
WL sent his sons there to learn to read and write. (6)
WL was ___-sick for Lotus. (4)
WL would not eat the ___ his 2nd son stole. (4)
WL's country (5)
WL's father would not do this. (3)
WL's first mistress (5)
Wang Lung's ___'s family stayed in the house (5)
When WL cut off his braid, O-lan said, 'You have cut off your ___!' (4)
Working on it made WL well again. (4)
___ Lung had a strong attachment to the land. (4)
___ a female child was an accepted means of survival for the poor. (7)

Good Earth Word Search 2 Answer Key

Words are placed backwards, forward, diagonally, up and down. Clues listed below can help you find the words. Circle the hidden vocabulary words in the maze.

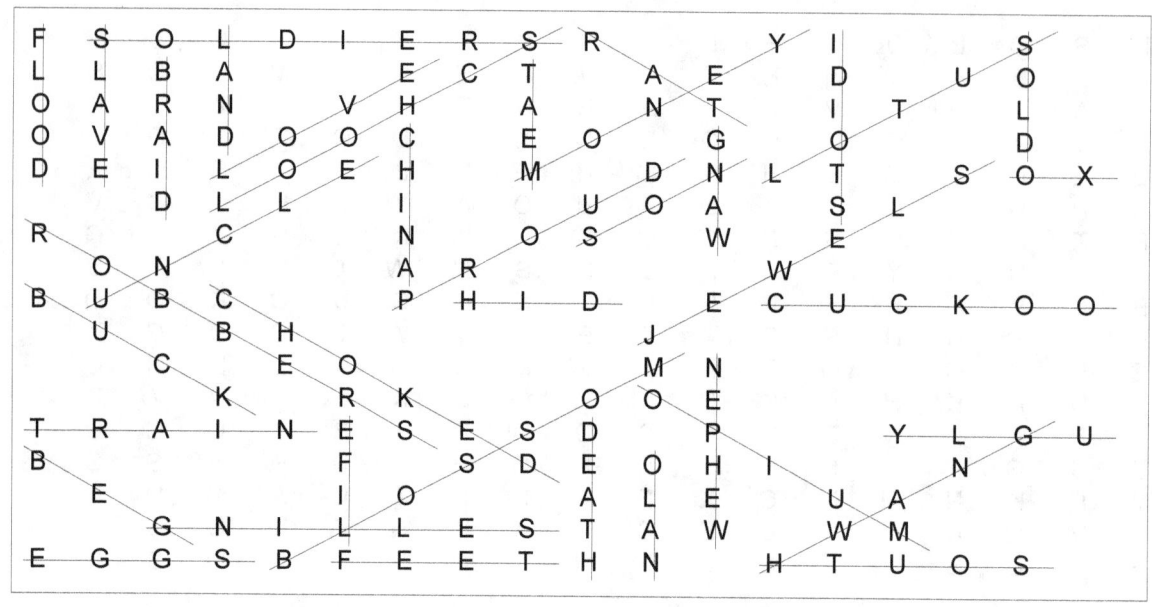

'He lived in the rich city as alien as a ___ in a rich man's house.' (3)
'When I return to that house it will be with my ___ in my arms.' (3)
A great ___ came. (water disaster) (5)
Author (4)
Characteristic of Wang Lung; he was ___. (5)
Direction WL wanted to go to find food and work (5)
He went to join the war & see the country. (6)
In the 7th year of prosperity, WL saw O-lan as ___. (4)
Lotus called WL's children this. (6)
O-lan ___ the newborn child; it would have died of starvation. (6)
O-lan bound her daughter's ___. (4)
O-lan had ___ hidden in the cloth. (6)
O-lan killed it for food. (2)
O-lan's final words to Cuckoo: '...you are still a ___.' (5)
Servant woman with whom WL bargained for land (6)
She married Wang Lung. (4)
She promised to take care of Wang Lung's daughter. (7)
The two sons ___ WL's land and divided the profits. (4)
The uncle belonged to a band of ___. (7)

They arrested poor men. (8)
To escape soldiers, WL ___ during the day. (3)
Transportation south (5)
WL bought land from the House of ___. (5)
WL claimed their child was a female with smallpox & prayed for its ___. (5)
WL cut off his ___. (5)
WL dyed these red and gave them to friends to celebrate the birth of his son. (4)
WL gave his uncle ___ to protect his own reputation. (5)
WL gave his uncle's family this to make them less of a nuisance. (5)
WL sent his sons there to learn to read and write. (6)
WL was ___-sick for Lotus. (4)
WL would not eat the ___ his 2nd son stole. (4)
WL's country (5)
WL's father would not do this. (3)
WL's first mistress (5)
Wang Lung's ___'s family stayed in the house (5)
When WL cut off his braid, O-lan said, 'You have cut off your ___!' (4)
Working on it made WL well again. (4)
___ Lung had a strong attachment to the land. (4)
___ a female child was an accepted means of survival for the poor. (7)

Good Earth Word Search 3

Words are placed backwards, forward, diagonally, up and down. Words listed below are included in the maze. Circle the hidden vocabulary words in the maze.

```
B R A I D U O R P F U R N I T U R E
C H D Y G O J N R F P S J J Z Y T X
J D R Y K D X Q T Q X L K S H S H Z
E S M C N J V A N D D A H F L S R Y
W Z U N E T E M N Z L V M L T K T C
E C K G P M S F Y G B E J O L P K S
L H T W H T C G S G R W I Y C X D R
S O B H E X S K O R K D F T R K V K
T K B H W H T L L K I B N C Y Y W M
B E Y R Q Y T B D Y K T D J H Z B P
X D Q N R P Y L I T C D Z R W R L M
B H A B S D P K E P R O B S A M O M
S L U K O F Z H R Z M O E E N U V L
O C H I N A M O S S O L B O G D E C
K T H L D O W R P O L F I L P G Q C
S R X O N B E A U I U P Y F O I S S
S A H E O B W J N R A T W L E X U Z
O I Y I B L K G C G H E H P A T M M
L N K O D D Z J L B J E Y V O N H M
D X R D E A T H E N H F T L M C D L
```

BEG	EGGS	LAND	OPIUM	SOLD
BLOSSOM	FEET	LIFE	OX	SOLDIERS
BRAID	FLOOD	LOTUS	PROUD	SON
BUCK	FURNITURE	LOVE	RAT	SOUTH
CHINA	HID	MEAT	ROBBERS	TRAIN
CHOKED	HWANG	MONEY	SCHOOL	UGLY
CUCKOO	IDIOTS	NEPHEW	SELLING	UNCLE
DEATH	JEWELS	OLAN	SLAVE	WANG

Good Earth Word Search 3 Answer Key

Words are placed backwards, forward, diagonally, up and down. Words listed below are included in the maze. Circle the hidden vocabulary words in the maze.

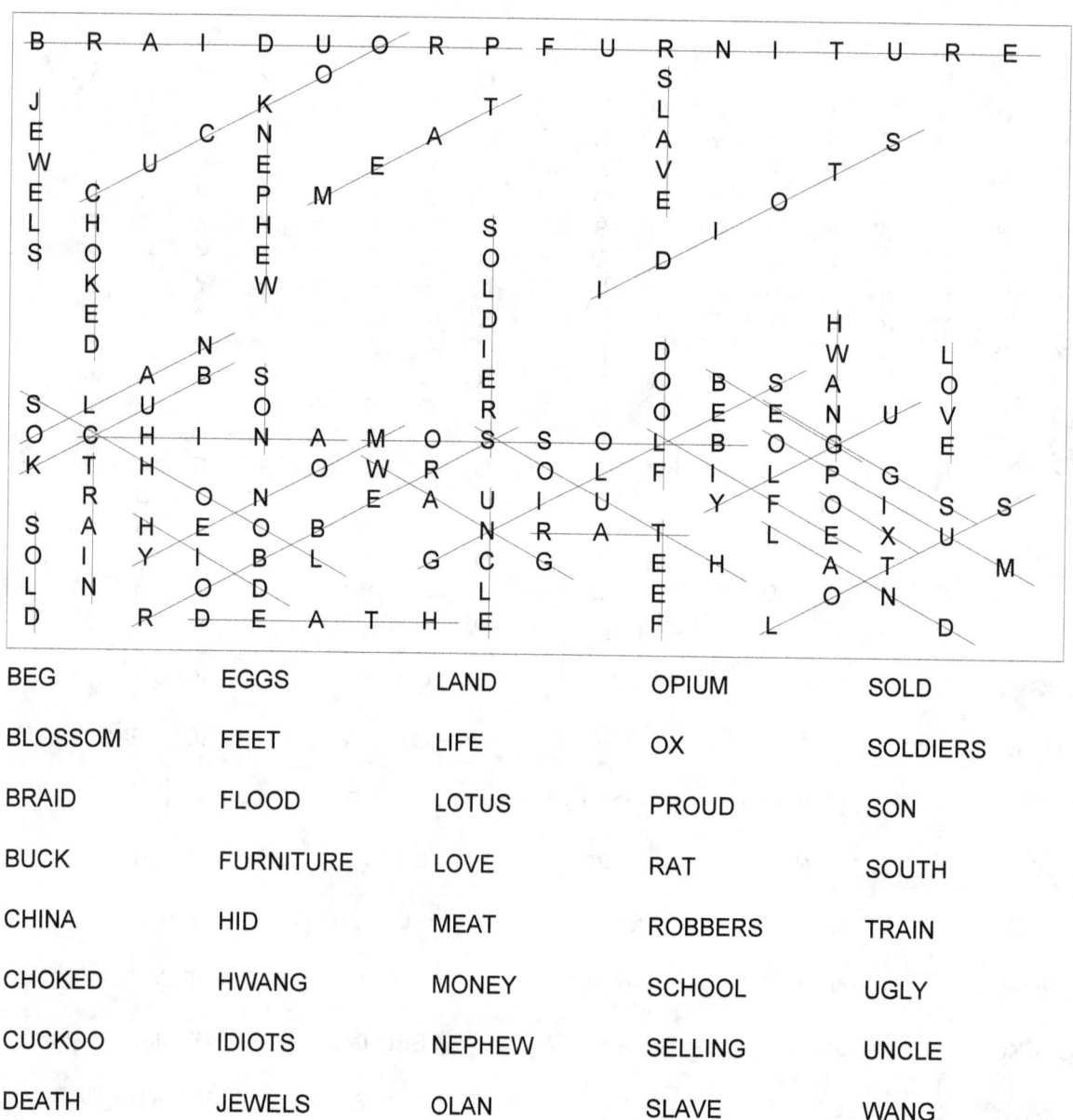

BEG	EGGS	LAND	OPIUM	SOLD
BLOSSOM	FEET	LIFE	OX	SOLDIERS
BRAID	FLOOD	LOTUS	PROUD	SON
BUCK	FURNITURE	LOVE	RAT	SOUTH
CHINA	HID	MEAT	ROBBERS	TRAIN
CHOKED	HWANG	MONEY	SCHOOL	UGLY
CUCKOO	IDIOTS	NEPHEW	SELLING	UNCLE
DEATH	JEWELS	OLAN	SLAVE	WANG

Good Earth Word Search 1

Words are placed backwards, forward, diagonally, up and down. Words listed below are included in the maze. Circle the hidden vocabulary words in the maze.

S	E	L	L	I	N	G	G	L	W	F	E	E	T	Y	C	J	X
O	O	N	D	V	M	D	X	K	A	L	P	S	Y	F	Z	G	H
U	P	L	L	H	Y	M	P	J	N	S	O	L	D	I	E	R	S
T	B	Z	D	F	Y	N	G	H	G	D	C	R	L	W	L	G	H
H	F	U	G	H	L	G	P	H	F	S	P	D	O	T	J	M	V
T	P	G	C	G	G	P	Y	T	J	D	S	Q	O	H	K	H	V
T	W	B	K	K	T	G	Y	M	B	Q	D	L	H	N	D	T	N
M	D	H	Z	X	B	F	H	T	L	M	F	R	C	X	S	C	N
J	L	K	Y	T	M	B	S	W	O	E	G	G	S	X	T	H	Q
T	H	B	M	G	X	L	B	M	S	V	S	O	O	N	O	O	C
T	T	R	K	R	A	F	L	E	S	Q	N	S	Z	E	I	K	Y
Z	A	N	B	V	T	U	K	A	O	O	H	R	C	P	D	E	T
J	E	W	E	L	S	R	A	T	M	O	N	E	Y	H	I	D	K
P	D	Z	G	B	T	N	A	W	M	K	L	B	V	E	I	G	F
R	P	K	S	S	R	I	N	I	K	C	R	B	H	W	N	N	P
O	P	F	X	T	L	T	G	D	N	U	Z	O	W	N	F	O	A
U	F	L	O	O	D	U	X	U	C	C	B	R	A	I	D	P	N
D	X	X	T	N	F	R	L	G	G	L	P	L	N	Z	F	I	F
G	H	U	A	N	D	E	Z	L	W	Z	O	P	G	F	H	U	H
F	S	L	I	F	E	V	F	Y	K	L	O	V	E	W	W	M	G

BEG	EGGS	LAND	OPIUM	SOLD
BLOSSOM	FEET	LIFE	OX	SOLDIERS
BRAID	FLOOD	LOTUS	PROUD	SON
BUCK	FURNITURE	LOVE	RAT	SOUTH
CHINA	HID	MEAT	ROBBERS	TRAIN
CHOKED	HWANG	MONEY	SCHOOL	UGLY
CUCKOO	IDIOTS	NEPHEW	SELLING	UNCLE
DEATH	JEWELS	OLAN	SLAVE	WANG

Good Earth Word Search 4 Answer Key

Words are placed backwards, forward, diagonally, up and down. Words listed below are included in the maze. Circle the hidden vocabulary words in the maze.

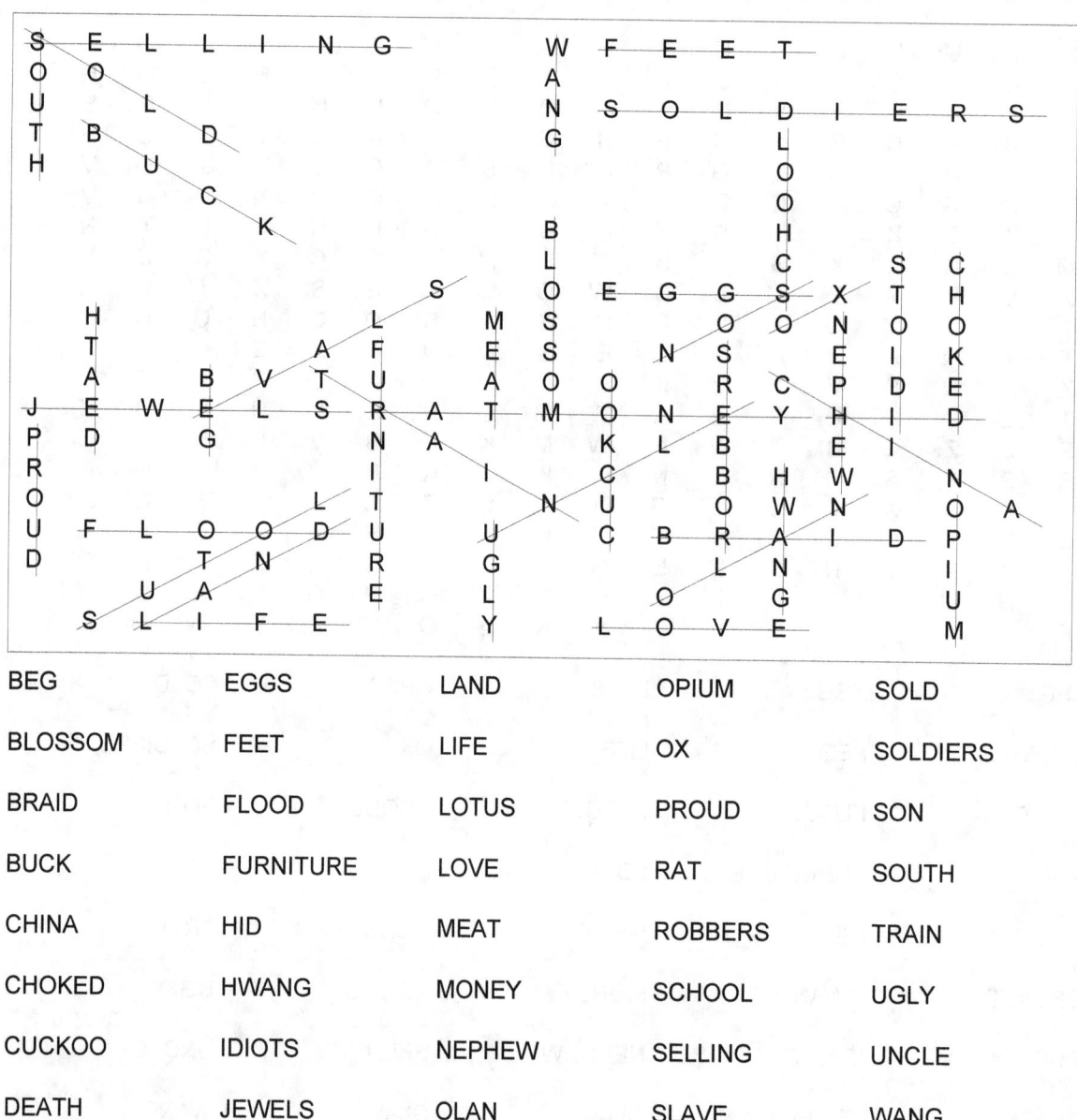

BEG	EGGS	LAND	OPIUM	SOLD
BLOSSOM	FEET	LIFE	OX	SOLDIERS
BRAID	FLOOD	LOTUS	PROUD	SON
BUCK	FURNITURE	LOVE	RAT	SOUTH
CHINA	HID	MEAT	ROBBERS	TRAIN
CHOKED	HWANG	MONEY	SCHOOL	UGLY
CUCKOO	IDIOTS	NEPHEW	SELLING	UNCLE
DEATH	JEWELS	OLAN	SLAVE	WANG

Good Earth Crossword 1

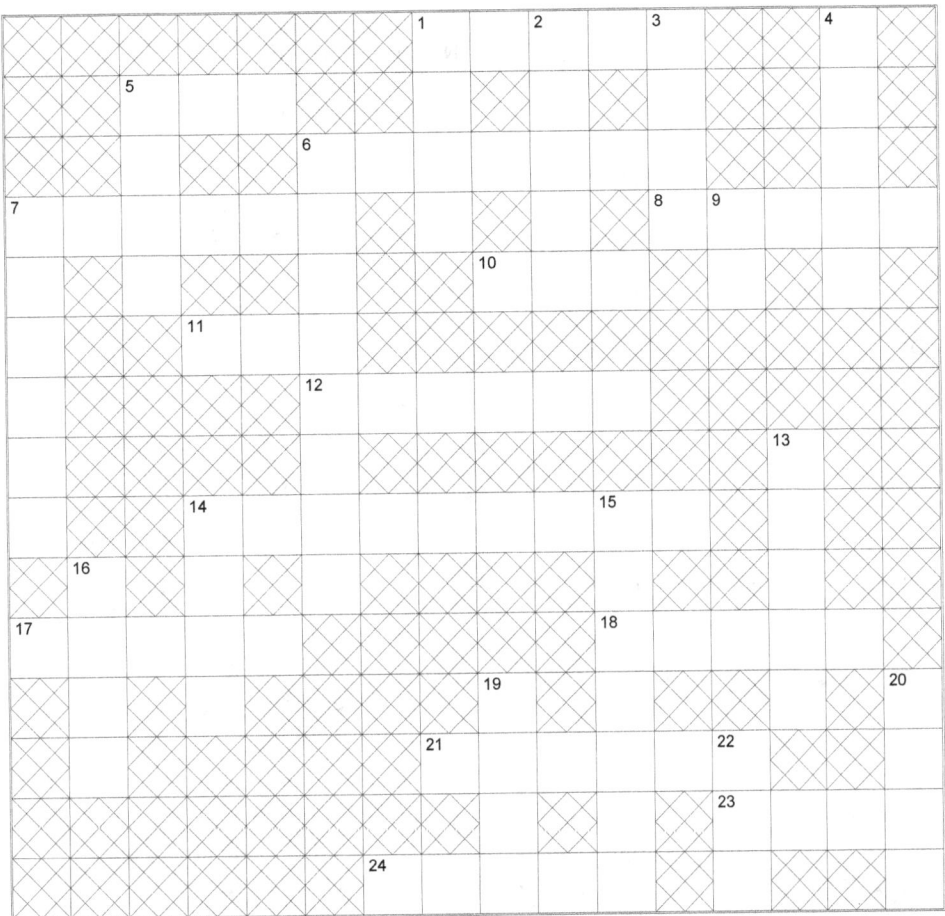

Across
1. Wang Lung's ___'s family stayed in the house
5. WL's father would not do this.
6. ___ a female child was an accepted means of survival for the poor.
7. Servant woman with whom WL bargained for land
8. Direction WL wanted to go to find food and work
10. 'He lived in the rich city as alien as a ___ in a rich man's house.'
11. To escape soldiers, WL ___ during the day.
12. Lotus called WL's children this.
14. WL sold his ___ to get money to go south.
17. WL gave his uncle ___ to protect his own reputation.
18. WL cut off his ___.
21. O-lan had ___ hidden in the cloth.
23. She married Wang Lung.
24. WL's first mistress

Down
1. In the 7th year of prosperity, WL saw O-lan as ___.
2. WL's country
3. WL dyed these red and gave them to friends to celebrate the birth of his son.
4. WL claimed their child was a female with smallpox & prayed for its ___.
5. Author
6. They arrested poor men.
7. O-lan ___ the newborn child; it would have died of starvation.
9. O-lan killed it for food.
13. Transportation south
14. O-lan bound her daughter's ___.
15. The uncle belonged to a band of ___.
16. The two sons ___ WL's land and divided the profits.
19. WL would not eat the ___ his 2nd son stole.
20. Working on it made WL well again.
22. 'When I return to that house it will be with my ___ in my arms.'

Good Earth Crossword 1 Answer Key

Across
1. Wang Lung's ___'s family stayed in the house
5. WL's father would not do this.
6. ___ a female child was an accepted means of survival for the poor.
7. Servant woman with whom WL bargained for land
8. Direction WL wanted to go to find food and work
10. 'He lived in the rich city as alien as a ___ in a rich man's house.'
11. To escape soldiers, WL ___ during the day.
12. Lotus called WL's children this.
14. WL sold his ___ to get money to go south.
17. WL gave his uncle ___ to protect his own reputation.
18. WL cut off his ___.
21. O-lan had ___ hidden in the cloth.
23. She married Wang Lung.
24. WL's first mistress

Down
1. In the 7th year of prosperity, WL saw O-lan as ___.
2. WL's country
3. WL dyed these red and gave them to friends to celebrate the birth of his son.
4. WL claimed their child was a female with smallpox & prayed for its ___.
5. Author
6. They arrested poor men.
7. O-lan ___ the newborn child; it would have died of starvation.
9. O-lan killed it for food.
13. Transportation south
14. O-lan bound her daughter's ___.
15. The uncle belonged to a band of ___.
16. The two sons ___ WL's land and divided the profits.
19. WL would not eat the ___ his 2nd son stole.
20. Working on it made WL well again.
22. 'When I return to that house it will be with my ___ in my arms.'

Good Earth Crossword 2

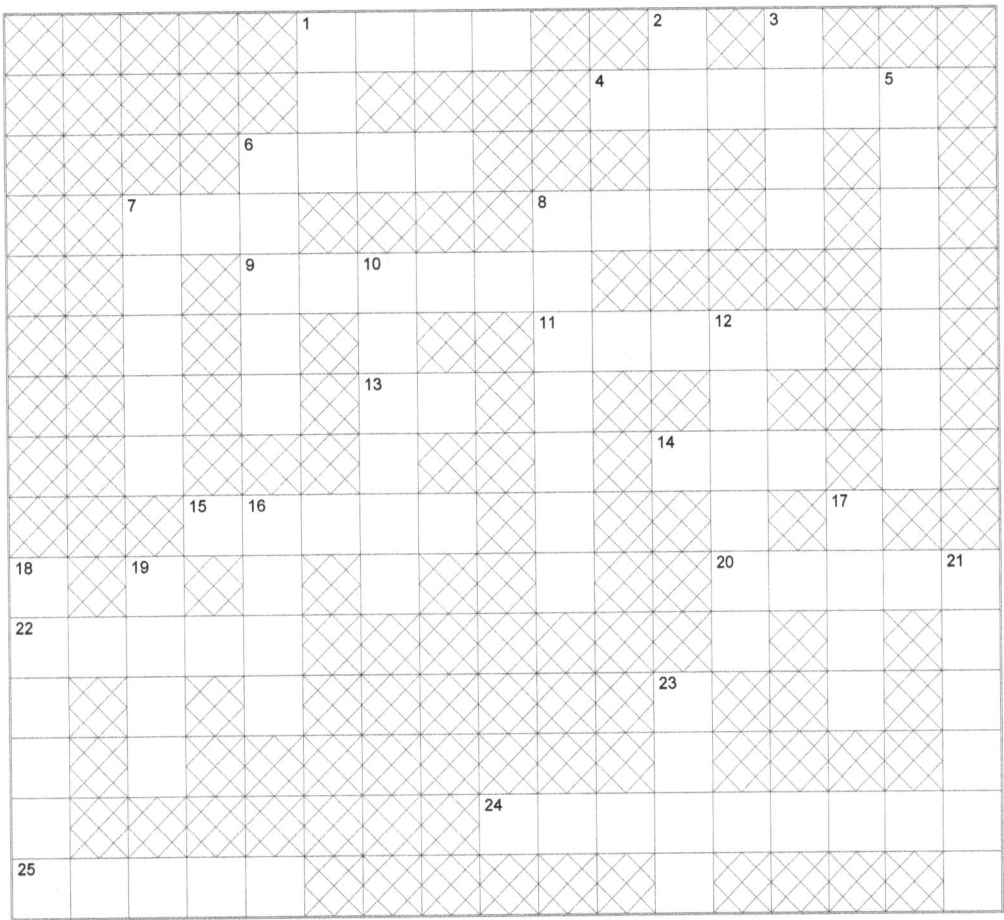

Across
1. Author
4. O-lan had ___ hidden in the cloth.
6. In the 7th year of prosperity, WL saw O-lan as ___.
7. 'When I return to that house it will be with my ___ in my arms.'
8. 'He lived in the rich city as alien as a ___ in a rich man's house.'
9. Servant woman with whom WL bargained for land
11. WL cut off his ___.
13. O-lan killed it for food.
14. To escape soldiers, WL ___ during the day.
15. WL gave his uncle ___ to protect his own reputation.
20. Transportation south
22. WL's country
24. WL sold his ___ to get money to go south.
25. WL's first mistress

Down
1. WL's father would not do this.
2. WL would not eat the ___ his 2nd son stole.
3. O-lan bound her daughter's ___.
5. ___ a female child was an accepted means of survival for the poor.
6. Wang Lung's ___'s family stayed in the house
7. Direction WL wanted to go to find food and work
8. The uncle belonged to a band of ___.
10. O-lan ___ the newborn child; it would have died of starvation.
12. Lotus called WL's children this.
16. She married Wang Lung.
17. Working on it made WL well again.
18. WL sent his sons there to learn to read and write.
19. When WL cut off his braid, O-lan said, 'You have cut off your ___!'
21. He went to join the war & see the country.
23. ___ Lung had a strong attachment to the land.

Good Earth Crossword 2 Answer Key

Across
1. Author
4. O-lan had ___ hidden in the cloth.
6. In the 7th year of prosperity, WL saw O-lan as ___.
7. 'When I return to that house it will be with my ___ in my arms.'
8. 'He lived in the rich city as alien as a ___ in a rich man's house.'
9. Servant woman with whom WL bargained for land
11. WL cut off his ___.
13. O-lan killed it for food.
14. To escape soldiers, WL ___ during the day.
15. WL gave his uncle ___ to protect his own reputation.
20. Transportation south
22. WL's country
24. WL sold his ___ to get money to go south.
25. WL's first mistress

Down
1. WL's father would not do this.
2. WL would not eat the ___ his 2nd son stole.
3. O-lan bound her daughter's ___.
5. ___ a female child was an accepted means of survival for the poor.
6. Wang Lung's ___'s family stayed in the house
7. Direction WL wanted to go to find food and work
8. The uncle belonged to a band of ___.
10. O-lan ___ the newborn child; it would have died of starvation.
12. Lotus called WL's children this.
16. She married Wang Lung.
17. Working on it made WL well again.
18. WL sent his sons there to learn to read and write.
19. When WL cut off his braid, O-lan said, 'You have cut off your ___!'
21. He went to join the war & see the country.
23. ___ Lung had a strong attachment to the land.

Good Earth Crossword 3

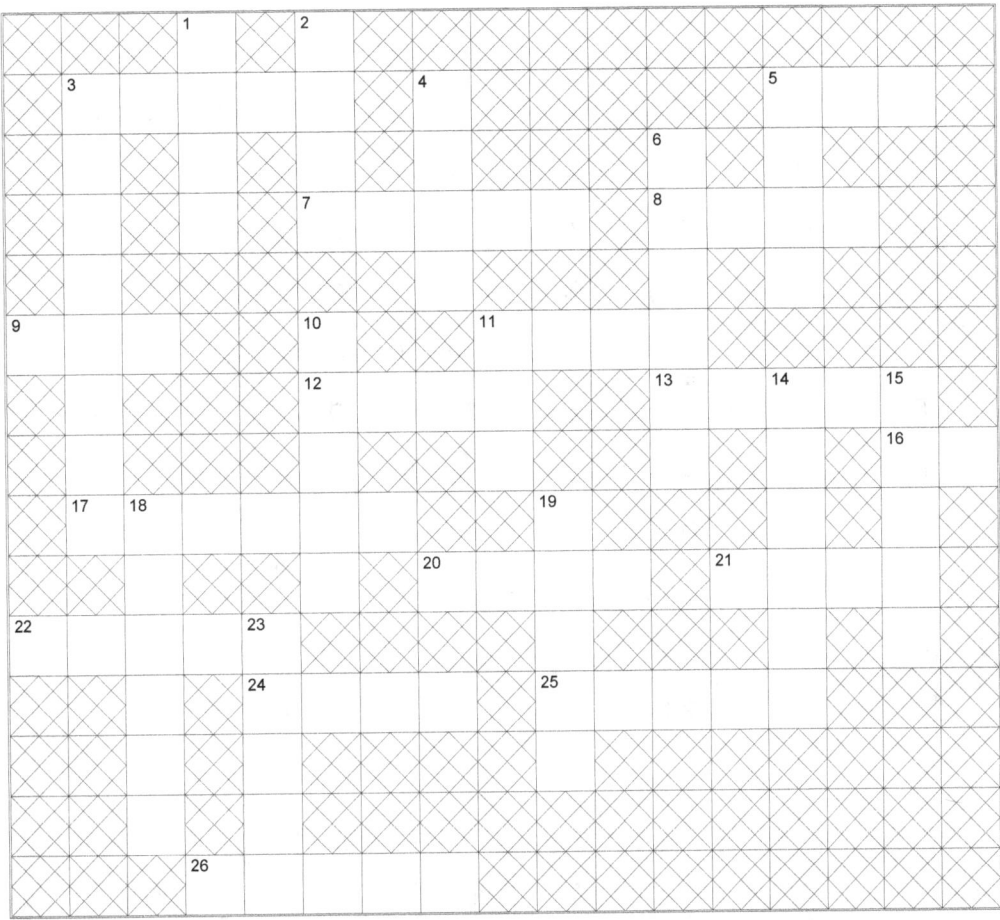

Across

3. O-lan's final words to Cuckoo: '...you are still a ___.'
5. 'When I return to that house it will be with my ___ in my arms.'
7. Transportation south
8. In the 7th year of prosperity, WL saw O-lan as ___.
9. To escape soldiers, WL ___ during the day.
11. Author
12. When WL cut off his braid, O-lan said, 'You have cut off your ___!'
13. WL gave his uncle's family this to make them less of a nuisance.
16. O-lan killed it for food.
17. WL sent his sons there to learn to read and write.
20. Working on it made WL well again.
21. WL was ___-sick for Lotus.
22. Characteristic of Wang Lung; he was ___.
24. WL dyed these red and gave them to friends to celebrate the birth of his son.
25. WL's first mistress
26. WL's country

Down

1. ___ Lung had a strong attachment to the land.
2. WL would not eat the ___ his 2nd son stole.
3. They arrested poor men.
4. She married Wang Lung.
5. The two sons ___ WL's land and divided the profits.
6. Servant woman with whom WL bargained for land
10. A great ___ came. (water disaster)
11. WL's father would not do this.
14. Lotus called WL's children this.
15. WL gave his uncle ___ to protect his own reputation.
18. O-lan ___ the newborn child; it would have died of starvation.
19. Wang Lung's ___'s family stayed in the house
23. WL claimed their child was a female with smallpox & prayed for its ___.

Good Earth Crossword 3 Answer Key

				1 W		2 M								
		3 S	L	A	V	E		4 O				5 S	O	N
		O		N		A		L			6 C	O		
		L		G		7 T	R	A	I	N	8 U	G	L	Y
		D				N					C		D	
9 H	I	D			10 F		11 B	U	C	K				
	E			12 L	I	F	E				13 O	P	14 U	15 M
	R			O			G				D			16 O	X
	17 S	18 C	H	O	O	L		19 U			I			N
		H			20 D		L	A	N	D		21 L	O	V	E
22 P	R	O	U	23 D				C				T		Y
		K		24 E	G	G	S		25 L	O	T	U	S	
		E		A					E					
		D		T										
				26 C	H	I	N	A						

Across

3. O-lan's final words to Cuckoo: '...you are still a ___.'
5. 'When I return to that house it will be with my ___ in my arms.'
7. Transportation south
8. In the 7th year of prosperity, WL saw O-lan as ___.
9. To escape soldiers, WL ___ during the day.
11. Author
12. When WL cut off his braid, O-lan said, 'You have cut off your ___!'
13. WL gave his uncle's family this to make them less of a nuisance.
16. O-lan killed it for food.
17. WL sent his sons there to learn to read and write.
20. Working on it made WL well again.
21. WL was ___-sick for Lotus.
22. Characteristic of Wang Lung; he was ___.
24. WL dyed these red and gave them to friends to celebrate the birth of his son.
25. WL's first mistress
26. WL's country

Down

1. ___ Lung had a strong attachment to the land.
2. WL would not eat the ___ his 2nd son stole.
3. They arrested poor men.
4. She married Wang Lung.
5. The two sons ___ WL's land and divided the profits.
6. Servant woman with whom WL bargained for land
10. A great ___ came. (water disaster)
11. WL's father would not do this.
14. Lotus called WL's children this.
15. WL gave his uncle ___ to protect his own reputation.
18. O-lan ___ the newborn child; it would have died of starvation.
19. Wang Lung's ___'s family stayed in the house
23. WL claimed their child was a female with smallpox & prayed for its ___.

Good Earth Crossword 4

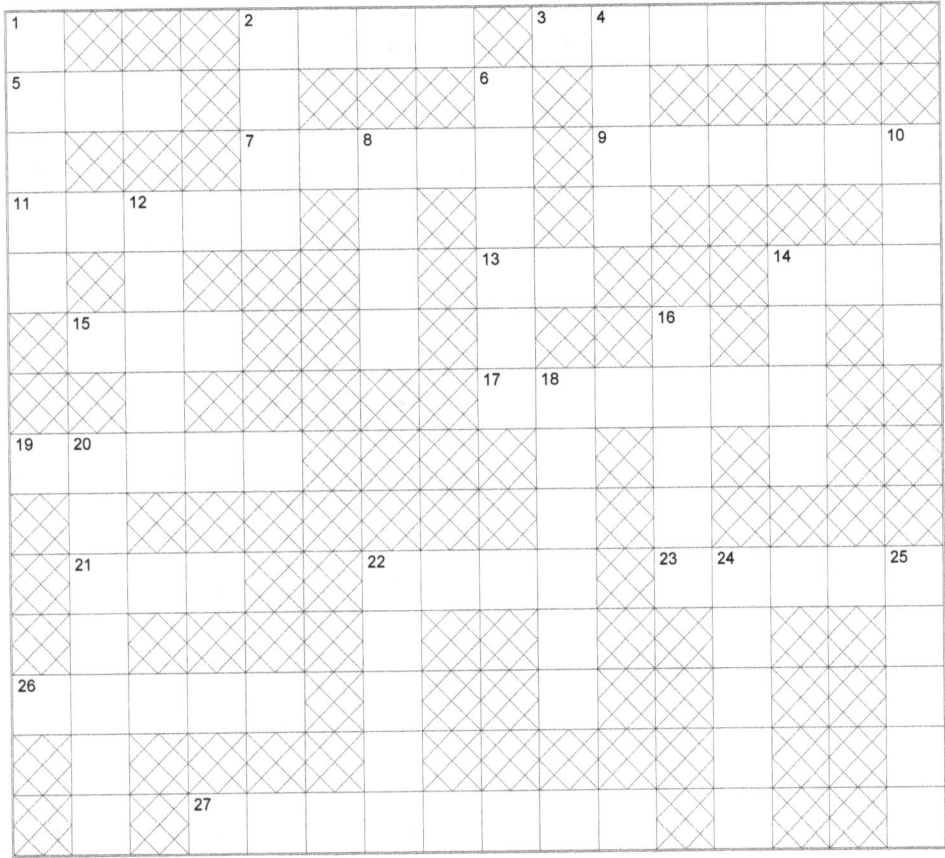

Across

2. WL was ___-sick for Lotus.
3. O-lan's final words to Cuckoo: '...you are still a ___.'
5. 'He lived in the rich city as alien as a ___ in a rich man's house.'
7. A great ___ came. (water disaster)
9. He went to join the war & see the country.
11. Wang Lung's ___'s family stayed in the house
13. O-lan killed it for food.
14. 'When I return to that house it will be with my ___ in my arms.'
15. To escape soldiers, WL ___ during the day.
17. WL sent his sons there to learn to read and write.
19. Transportation south
21. WL's father would not do this.
22. Author
23. Direction WL wanted to go to find food and work
26. WL claimed their child was a female with smallpox & prayed for its ___.
27. They arrested poor men.

Down

1. Characteristic of Wang Lung; he was ___.
2. When WL cut off his braid, O-lan said, 'You have cut off your ___!'
4. Working on it made WL well again.
6. Lotus called WL's children this.
8. She married Wang Lung.
10. ___ Lung had a strong attachment to the land.
12. WL's country
14. The two sons ___ WL's land and divided the profits.
16. WL's first mistress
18. Servant woman with whom WL bargained for land
20. The uncle belonged to a band of ___.
22. WL cut off his ___.
24. WL gave his uncle's family this to make them less of a nuisance.
25. WL bought land from the House of ___.

Good Earth Crossword 4 Answer Key

		1 P				2 L	O	V	E		3 S	4 L	A	V	E
		5 R	A	T		I				6 I		A			
		O			7 F	L	8 O	O	D		9 N	E	P	H	10 W
	11 U	N	12 C	L	E		L		I		D				A
		D		H			A		13 O	X			14 S	O	N
			15 H	I	D		N		T			16 L	O	G	
				N				17 S	18 C	H	O	O	L		
19 T	20 R	A	I	N					U		T		D		
	O								C		U				
	21 B	E	G			22 B	U	C	K		23 S	24 O	U	T	25 H
	B					R			O			P			W
26 D	E	A	T	H		A			O			I			A
	R					I						U			N
	S		27 S	O	L	D	I	E	R	S		M			G

Across
2. WL was ___-sick for Lotus.
3. O-lan's final words to Cuckoo: '...you are still a ___.'
5. 'He lived in the rich city as alien as a ___ in a rich man's house.'
7. A great ___ came. (water disaster)
9. He went to join the war & see the country.
11. Wang Lung's ___'s family stayed in the house
13. O-lan killed it for food.
14. 'When I return to that house it will be with my ___ in my arms.'
15. To escape soldiers, WL ___ during the day.
17. WL sent his sons there to learn to read and write.
19. Transportation south
21. WL's father would not do this.
22. Author
23. Direction WL wanted to go to find food and work
26. WL claimed their child was a female with smallpox & prayed for its ___.
27. They arrested poor men.

Down
1. Characteristic of Wang Lung; he was ___.
2. When WL cut off his braid, O-lan said, 'You have cut off your ___!'
4. Working on it made WL well again.
6. Lotus called WL's children this.
8. She married Wang Lung.
10. ___ Lung had a strong attachment to the land.
12. WL's country
14. The two sons ___ WL's land and divided the profits.
16. WL's first mistress
18. Servant woman with whom WL bargained for land
20. The uncle belonged to a band of ___.
22. WL cut off his ___.
24. WL gave his uncle's family this to make them less of a nuisance.
25. WL bought land from the House of ___.

Good Earth

BLOSSOM	FLOOD	UGLY	LOTUS	OPIUM
FURNITURE	CHOKED	SELLING	SCHOOL	BRAID
LIFE	TRAIN	FREE SPACE	UNCLE	FEET
LOVE	HID	ROBBERS	HWANG	OX
BEG	EGGS	SLAVE	CUCKOO	BUCK

Good Earth

SOLDIERS	LAND	WANG	IDIOTS	MEAT
JEWELS	SON	NEPHEW	SOLD	PROUD
DEATH	OLAN	FREE SPACE	MONEY	SOUTH
BUCK	CUCKOO	SLAVE	EGGS	BEG
OX	HWANG	ROBBERS	HID	LOVE

45
Copyrighted

Good Earth

SLAVE	LAND	PROUD	MEAT	FLOOD
LOTUS	FURNITURE	TRAIN	RAT	NEPHEW
SON	SOLDIERS	FREE SPACE	FEET	OX
UGLY	MONEY	HID	EGGS	CUCKOO
BLOSSOM	HWANG	OPIUM	CHINA	BRAID

Good Earth

SOUTH	ROBBERS	UNCLE	BEG	IDIOTS
LOVE	SELLING	LIFE	OLAN	BUCK
SCHOOL	WANG	FREE SPACE	SOLD	JEWELS
BRAID	CHINA	OPIUM	HWANG	BLOSSOM
CUCKOO	EGGS	HID	MONEY	UGLY

Good Earth

BUCK	LIFE	FURNITURE	NEPHEW	ROBBERS
SCHOOL	SELLING	LOTUS	MEAT	OX
BRAID	JEWELS	FREE SPACE	CUCKOO	SOLD
BLOSSOM	IDIOTS	DEATH	OPIUM	OLAN
PROUD	FLOOD	CHOKED	SOLDIERS	FEET

Good Earth

MONEY	BEG	EGGS	TRAIN	SOUTH
HID	SLAVE	RAT	UNCLE	UGLY
WANG	LOVE	FREE SPACE	LAND	SON
FEET	SOLDIERS	CHOKED	FLOOD	PROUD
OLAN	OPIUM	DEATH	IDIOTS	BLOSSOM

Good Earth

CUCKOO	BRAID	JEWELS	DEATH	SOUTH
NEPHEW	UNCLE	SOLDIERS	OPIUM	FEET
LOVE	MONEY	FREE SPACE	SLAVE	HWANG
CHOKED	IDIOTS	CHINA	SOLD	MEAT
LAND	EGGS	BLOSSOM	PROUD	RAT

Good Earth

FURNITURE	UGLY	TRAIN	LOTUS	BUCK
SON	ROBBERS	HID	WANG	OLAN
LIFE	BEG	FREE SPACE	FLOOD	SCHOOL
RAT	PROUD	BLOSSOM	EGGS	LAND
MEAT	SOLD	CHINA	IDIOTS	CHOKED

Good Earth

CUCKOO	PROUD	UNCLE	LOTUS	LIFE
HID	OX	SCHOOL	BLOSSOM	SOUTH
CHOKED	EGGS	FREE SPACE	MONEY	SELLING
OLAN	UGLY	HWANG	SON	OPIUM
CHINA	FEET	MEAT	WANG	BRAID

Good Earth

NEPHEW	BEG	SOLDIERS	BUCK	LAND
JEWELS	DEATH	FURNITURE	FLOOD	TRAIN
SOLD	ROBBERS	FREE SPACE	SLAVE	IDIOTS
BRAID	WANG	MEAT	FEET	CHINA
OPIUM	SON	HWANG	UGLY	OLAN

Good Earth

SOLDIERS	LIFE	RAT	OX	SCHOOL
LOVE	SOLD	HID	FEET	LOTUS
UNCLE	CHOKED	FREE SPACE	OPIUM	BUCK
IDIOTS	NEPHEW	MEAT	SON	DEATH
BRAID	HWANG	MONEY	WANG	TRAIN

Good Earth

SLAVE	FURNITURE	FLOOD	CUCKOO	CHINA
BEG	LAND	UGLY	JEWELS	EGGS
ROBBERS	PROUD	FREE SPACE	BLOSSOM	SOUTH
TRAIN	WANG	MONEY	HWANG	BRAID
DEATH	SON	MEAT	NEPHEW	IDIOTS

Good Earth

BRAID	OPIUM	SCHOOL	OX	UNCLE
FLOOD	HID	UGLY	WANG	SON
IDIOTS	DEATH	FREE SPACE	SOLDIERS	FURNITURE
LIFE	PROUD	BUCK	RAT	BEG
TRAIN	JEWELS	CHOKED	OLAN	MEAT

Good Earth

EGGS	LOVE	FEET	MONEY	SOLD
ROBBERS	HWANG	LAND	SLAVE	CUCKOO
NEPHEW	BLOSSOM	FREE SPACE	SELLING	LOTUS
MEAT	OLAN	CHOKED	JEWELS	TRAIN
BEG	RAT	BUCK	PROUD	LIFE

Good Earth

SELLING	EGGS	SOUTH	IDIOTS	CHOKED
BEG	BUCK	SON	UGLY	LIFE
HID	JEWELS	FREE SPACE	SLAVE	OX
SOLDIERS	SOLD	CHINA	BLOSSOM	MEAT
PROUD	OPIUM	MONEY	HWANG	TRAIN

Good Earth

LOVE	RAT	FEET	ROBBERS	BRAID
FLOOD	WANG	SCHOOL	CUCKOO	FURNITURE
OLAN	LAND	FREE SPACE	UNCLE	LOTUS
TRAIN	HWANG	MONEY	OPIUM	PROUD
MEAT	BLOSSOM	CHINA	SOLD	SOLDIERS

Good Earth

SON	MONEY	BLOSSOM	MEAT	IDIOTS
NEPHEW	JEWELS	CUCKOO	SELLING	SCHOOL
HWANG	LIFE	FREE SPACE	OPIUM	OX
FEET	WANG	EGGS	RAT	BUCK
LOVE	LOTUS	CHINA	SOLDIERS	SOUTH

Good Earth

FURNITURE	UGLY	HID	TRAIN	ROBBERS
BRAID	PROUD	UNCLE	FLOOD	CHOKED
OLAN	LAND	FREE SPACE	SLAVE	DEATH
SOUTH	SOLDIERS	CHINA	LOTUS	LOVE
BUCK	RAT	EGGS	WANG	FEET

Good Earth

IDIOTS	TRAIN	OX	OLAN	PROUD
BLOSSOM	BUCK	SELLING	EGGS	FURNITURE
JEWELS	LAND	FREE SPACE	SON	SOLD
HID	SLAVE	MEAT	SCHOOL	BEG
FLOOD	SOLDIERS	UNCLE	MONEY	DEATH

Good Earth

CHOKED	BRAID	CHINA	HWANG	NEPHEW
ROBBERS	SOUTH	UGLY	CUCKOO	OPIUM
LIFE	LOVE	FREE SPACE	LOTUS	RAT
DEATH	MONEY	UNCLE	SOLDIERS	FLOOD
BEG	SCHOOL	MEAT	SLAVE	HID

Good Earth

LIFE	EGGS	BLOSSOM	BEG	RAT
CUCKOO	IDIOTS	LOVE	DEATH	OPIUM
SOLDIERS	MONEY	FREE SPACE	LOTUS	CHOKED
ROBBERS	JEWELS	OLAN	SOLD	NEPHEW
OX	SON	SCHOOL	SLAVE	SOUTH

Good Earth

BRAID	SELLING	HID	PROUD	TRAIN
FURNITURE	FEET	UNCLE	CHINA	BUCK
UGLY	LAND	FREE SPACE	WANG	MEAT
SOUTH	SLAVE	SCHOOL	SON	OX
NEPHEW	SOLD	OLAN	JEWELS	ROBBERS

Good Earth

WANG	SON	FLOOD	LOTUS	BLOSSOM
UNCLE	NEPHEW	UGLY	IDIOTS	TRAIN
OLAN	SOUTH	FREE SPACE	FEET	HWANG
BEG	CHOKED	SOLD	RAT	CUCKOO
SCHOOL	PROUD	SOLDIERS	HID	CHINA

Good Earth

MEAT	MONEY	BUCK	OPIUM	ROBBERS
LIFE	OX	BRAID	DEATH	LOVE
JEWELS	EGGS	FREE SPACE	SLAVE	FURNITURE
CHINA	HID	SOLDIERS	PROUD	SCHOOL
CUCKOO	RAT	SOLD	CHOKED	BEG

Good Earth

IDIOTS	PROUD	BLOSSOM	SOLD	HID
DEATH	MONEY	LAND	BEG	EGGS
FLOOD	TRAIN	FREE SPACE	JEWELS	LOTUS
SCHOOL	ROBBERS	FEET	LIFE	OX
HWANG	SOLDIERS	LOVE	SELLING	SON

Good Earth

BRAID	SOUTH	NEPHEW	SLAVE	CHOKED
WANG	OLAN	CUCKOO	RAT	BUCK
FURNITURE	MEAT	FREE SPACE	OPIUM	UGLY
SON	SELLING	LOVE	SOLDIERS	HWANG
OX	LIFE	FEET	ROBBERS	SCHOOL

Good Earth

EGGS	OLAN	UNCLE	SON	CHINA
JEWELS	FEET	HWANG	BUCK	MEAT
TRAIN	SLAVE	FREE SPACE	PROUD	MONEY
SOLD	CUCKOO	HID	DEATH	BRAID
FLOOD	SCHOOL	ROBBERS	BLOSSOM	NEPHEW

Good Earth

RAT	LOVE	OPIUM	CHOKED	SOUTH
UGLY	OX	WANG	SOLDIERS	FURNITURE
LAND	IDIOTS	FREE SPACE	LIFE	LOTUS
NEPHEW	BLOSSOM	ROBBERS	SCHOOL	FLOOD
BRAID	DEATH	HID	CUCKOO	SOLD

Good Earth

SCHOOL	CUCKOO	MONEY	IDIOTS	BRAID
CHOKED	OLAN	DEATH	MEAT	SON
SELLING	TRAIN	FREE SPACE	UGLY	BEG
SLAVE	CHINA	OPIUM	HWANG	UNCLE
OX	BLOSSOM	WANG	LAND	FLOOD

Good Earth

SOLD	SOUTH	LIFE	EGGS	FEET
PROUD	JEWELS	FURNITURE	LOVE	HID
SOLDIERS	ROBBERS	FREE SPACE	RAT	LOTUS
FLOOD	LAND	WANG	BLOSSOM	OX
UNCLE	HWANG	OPIUM	CHINA	SLAVE

Good Earth

ROBBERS	DEATH	TRAIN	BEG	WANG
SON	UGLY	RAT	FEET	BLOSSOM
IDIOTS	HID	FREE SPACE	OPIUM	EGGS
MONEY	UNCLE	NEPHEW	CHINA	MEAT
BUCK	SCHOOL	SOLDIERS	OLAN	FLOOD

Good Earth

SOLD	SOUTH	PROUD	CUCKOO	CHOKED
FURNITURE	OX	JEWELS	LOVE	BRAID
SELLING	LAND	FREE SPACE	SLAVE	HWANG
FLOOD	OLAN	SOLDIERS	SCHOOL	BUCK
MEAT	CHINA	NEPHEW	UNCLE	MONEY

Good Earth Vocabulary Word List

No.	Word	Clue/Definition
1.	ACQUIESCENT	Passively agreeable
2.	AGAPE	In a state of wonder or amazement
3.	ARDENT	Passionate; full of strong feeling or enthusiasm
4.	ARDUOUS	Difficult
5.	BEGRUDGED	Gave reluctantly or resentfully
6.	BERATE	Reprimand; scold
7.	BLEARY	Blurred and/or reddened
8.	BOISTEROUSLY	Loudly; without restraint
9.	CLAD	Clothed
10.	COMPELLED	Forced
11.	CONCUBINES	Women contracted as second wives
12.	CONSTERNATION	State of paralyzing dismay
13.	CONTRIVED	Devised; planned; managed
14.	COQUETRY	Flirting
15.	COWERING	Cringing in fear
16.	DAIS	Raised platform
17.	DALLIED	Tarried; loitered; also means flirted
18.	DEMURRED	Objected
19.	DEPRECIATION	Making less of something
20.	DISTRAUGHT	Emotionally upset
21.	EMINENCE	Position of superiority
22.	FRUGAL	Thrifty; tight with money
23.	IDLE	Inactive; not working; being lazy
24.	IMPERTURBABLE	Unshakable; calm and steady
25.	IMPORTUNING	Persistently pleading
26.	IMPUDENT	Bold and offensive
27.	INCESSANT	Continuous
28.	LANGUOR	Lack of energy; listlessness
29.	LOATH	Reluctant
30.	LOWED	Mooed
31.	MALICE	Intent of ill-will
32.	MUSING	Considering thoughtfully
33.	OBEISANCES	Gestures of homage, deference, or reverence
34.	OPULENT	Having or showing great wealth
35.	PAGODA	Multi-story Buddhist tower
36.	PEEVISHLY	In a contrary way
37.	PETULANT	Unreasonably ill-tempered
38.	PITEOUS	Deserving pity
39.	PURGED	Purified; rid of undesirable elements
40.	QUERULOUSLY	Grumblingly; complainingly
41.	QUIESCENT	Quiet; still; inactive
42.	REAPED	Harvested; cut and collected
43.	REMORSE	Bitter regret
44.	REPINE	To be discontented or low in spirits
45.	RICKSHA	Small, two-wheeled carriage pulled by 1 or 2 people
46.	ROBUST	Full of strength and energy
47.	SCRUPULOUS	Conscientious; exact
48.	SHREWISH	Ill-humored
49.	SLAVISHLY	Like a slave
50.	SUPPED	Ate
51.	SURLY	Gruff

Good Earth Vocabulary Word List Continued

No.	Word	Clue/Definition
52.	UNCTUOUS	Slick; characterized by insincere earnestness
53.	VIRTUOUSLY	Showing moral excellence, virtue, or chastity
54.	VOLUBLY	Characterized by fluent speech
55.	WIZENED	Withered; wrinkled
56.	WRITHE	Twist; squirm; contort
57.	YEARN	To long for; to have feelings of tenderness for
58.	ZENITH	Highest point

Good Earth Vocabulary Fill In The Blanks 1

_____ 1. Passionate; full of strong feeling or enthusiasm

_____ 2. Harvested; cut and collected

_____ 3. Intent of ill-will

_____ 4. Conscientious; exact

_____ 5. Thrifty; tight with money

_____ 6. Considering thoughtfully

_____ 7. Ill-humored

_____ 8. Devised; planned; managed

_____ 9. Reprimand; scold

_____ 10. Reluctant

_____ 11. Lack of energy; listlessness

_____ 12. Characterized by fluent speech

_____ 13. In a contrary way

_____ 14. Inactive; not working; being lazy

_____ 15. In a state of wonder or amazement

_____ 16. Having or showing great wealth

_____ 17. Position of superiority

_____ 18. Unreasonably ill-tempered

_____ 19. Gave reluctantly or resentfully

_____ 20. State of paralyzing dismay

Good Earth Vocabulary Fill In The Blanks 1 Answer Key

ARDENT	1. Passionate; full of strong feeling or enthusiasm
REAPED	2. Harvested; cut and collected
MALICE	3. Intent of ill-will
SCRUPULOUS	4. Conscientious; exact
FRUGAL	5. Thrifty; tight with money
MUSING	6. Considering thoughtfully
SHREWISH	7. Ill-humored
CONTRIVED	8. Devised; planned; managed
BERATE	9. Reprimand; scold
LOATH	10. Reluctant
LANGUOR	11. Lack of energy; listlessness
VOLUBLY	12. Characterized by fluent speech
PEEVISHLY	13. In a contrary way
IDLE	14. Inactive; not working; being lazy
AGAPE	15. In a state of wonder or amazement
OPULENT	16. Having or showing great wealth
EMINENCE	17. Position of superiority
PETULANT	18. Unreasonably ill-tempered
BEGRUDGED	19. Gave reluctantly or resentfully
CONSTERNATION	20. State of paralyzing dismay

Good Earth Vocabulary Fill In The Blanks 2

_____ 1. To long for; to have feelings of tenderness for

_____ 2. Passively agreeable

_____ 3. Gestures of homage, deference, or reverence

_____ 4. Devised; planned; managed

_____ 5. Conscientious; exact

_____ 6. Ate

_____ 7. Slick; characterized by insincere earnestness

_____ 8. Lack of energy; listlessness

_____ 9. Clothed

_____ 10. Having or showing great wealth

_____ 11. In a contrary way

_____ 12. Characterized by fluent speech

_____ 13. Tarried; loitered; also means flirted

_____ 14. To be discontented or low in spirits

_____ 15. Withered; wrinkled

_____ 16. Objected

_____ 17. In a state of wonder or amazement

_____ 18. Considering thoughtfully

_____ 19. Quiet; still; inactive

_____ 20. Raised platform

Good Earth Vocabulary Fill In The Blanks 2 Answer Key

YEARN	1. To long for; to have feelings of tenderness for
ACQUIESCENT	2. Passively agreeable
OBEISANCES	3. Gestures of homage, deference, or reverence
CONTRIVED	4. Devised; planned; managed
SCRUPULOUS	5. Conscientious; exact
SUPPED	6. Ate
UNCTUOUS	7. Slick; characterized by insincere earnestness
LANGUOR	8. Lack of energy; listlessness
CLAD	9. Clothed
OPULENT	10. Having or showing great wealth
PEEVISHLY	11. In a contrary way
VOLUBLY	12. Characterized by fluent speech
DALLIED	13. Tarried; loitered; also means flirted
REPINE	14. To be discontented or low in spirits
WIZENED	15. Withered; wrinkled
DEMURRED	16. Objected
AGAPE	17. In a state of wonder or amazement
MUSING	18. Considering thoughtfully
QUIESCENT	19. Quiet; still; inactive
DAIS	20. Raised platform

Good Earth Vocabulary Fill In The Blanks 3

_____ 1. Grumblingly; complainingly

_____ 2. Forced

_____ 3. Cringing in fear

_____ 4. Twist; squirm; contort

_____ 5. Bitter regret

_____ 6. Difficult

_____ 7. Reprimand; scold

_____ 8. Gave reluctantly or resentfully

_____ 9. Gestures of homage, deference, or reverence

_____ 10. Women contracted as second wives

_____ 11. Characterized by fluent speech

_____ 12. Small, two-wheeled carriage pulled by 1 or 2 people

_____ 13. Conscientious; exact

_____ 14. Having or showing great wealth

_____ 15. Devised; planned; managed

_____ 16. Showing moral excellence, virtue, or chastity

_____ 17. Loudly; without restraint

_____ 18. Unshakable; calm and steady

_____ 19. Persistently pleading

_____ 20. Intent of ill-will

Good Earth Vocabulary Fill In The Blanks 3 Answer Key

QUERULOUSLY	1. Grumblingly; complainingly
COMPELLED	2. Forced
COWERING	3. Cringing in fear
WRITHE	4. Twist; squirm; contort
REMORSE	5. Bitter regret
ARDUOUS	6. Difficult
BERATE	7. Reprimand; scold
BEGRUDGED	8. Gave reluctantly or resentfully
OBEISANCES	9. Gestures of homage, deference, or reverence
CONCUBINES	10. Women contracted as second wives
VOLUBLY	11. Characterized by fluent speech
RICKSHA	12. Small, two-wheeled carriage pulled by 1 or 2 people
SCRUPULOUS	13. Conscientious; exact
OPULENT	14. Having or showing great wealth
CONTRIVED	15. Devised; planned; managed
VIRTUOUSLY	16. Showing moral excellence, virtue, or chastity
BOISTEROUSLY	17. Loudly; without restraint
IMPERTURBABLE	18. Unshakable; calm and steady
IMPORTUNING	19. Persistently pleading
MALICE	20. Intent of ill-will

Good Earth Vocabulary Fill In The Blanks 4

1. Inactive; not working; being lazy
2. Full of strength and energy
3. Quiet; still; inactive
4. Continuous
5. Passively agreeable
6. Lack of energy; listlessness
7. Position of superiority
8. In a contrary way
9. Cringing in fear
10. Making less of something
11. Women contracted as second wives
12. Clothed
13. Raised platform
14. Tarried; loitered; also means flirted
15. Like a slave
16. Unreasonably ill-tempered
17. Conscientious; exact
18. Blurred and/or reddened
19. Bitter regret
20. Gestures of homage, deference, or reverence

Good Earth Vocabulary Fill In The Blanks 4 Answer Key

IDLE	1. Inactive; not working; being lazy
ROBUST	2. Full of strength and energy
QUIESCENT	3. Quiet; still; inactive
INCESSANT	4. Continuous
ACQUIESCENT	5. Passively agreeable
LANGUOR	6. Lack of energy; listlessness
EMINENCE	7. Position of superiority
PEEVISHLY	8. In a contrary way
COWERING	9. Cringing in fear
DEPRECIATION	10. Making less of something
CONCUBINES	11. Women contracted as second wives
CLAD	12. Clothed
DAIS	13. Raised platform
DALLIED	14. Tarried; loitered; also means flirted
SLAVISHLY	15. Like a slave
PETULANT	16. Unreasonably ill-tempered
SCRUPULOUS	17. Conscientious; exact
BLEARY	18. Blurred and/or reddened
REMORSE	19. Bitter regret
OBEISANCES	20. Gestures of homage, deference, or reverence

Good Earth Vocabulary Matching 1

___ 1. IDLE
___ 2. CONTRIVED
___ 3. SLAVISHLY
___ 4. DALLIED
___ 5. OPULENT
___ 6. DEMURRED
___ 7. QUIESCENT
___ 8. IMPORTUNING
___ 9. LOATH
___ 10. LANGUOR
___ 11. PURGED
___ 12. PITEOUS
___ 13. AGAPE
___ 14. SUPPED
___ 15. REAPED
___ 16. FRUGAL
___ 17. DISTRAUGHT
___ 18. DEPRECIATION
___ 19. WRITHE
___ 20. PEEVISHLY
___ 21. UNCTUOUS
___ 22. VOLUBLY
___ 23. MUSING
___ 24. REPINE
___ 25. COMPELLED

A. Considering thoughtfully
B. Objected
C. In a state of wonder or amazement
D. Thrifty; tight with money
E. Having or showing great wealth
F. To be discontented or low in spirits
G. Inactive; not working; being lazy
H. Persistently pleading
I. Ate
J. Reluctant
K. Emotionally upset
L. Purified; rid of undesirable elements
M. Slick; characterized by insincere earnestness
N. Devised; planned; managed
O. Making less of something
P. Lack of energy; listlessness
Q. Deserving pity
R. Twist; squirm; contort
S. Characterized by fluent speech
T. Like a slave
U. In a contrary way
V. Tarried; loitered; also means flirted
W. Harvested; cut and collected
X. Forced
Y. Quiet; still; inactive

Good Earth Vocabulary Matching 1 Answer Key

G - 1. IDLE   A. Considering thoughtfully
N - 2. CONTRIVED   B. Objected
T - 3. SLAVISHLY   C. In a state of wonder or amazement
V - 4. DALLIED   D. Thrifty; tight with money
E - 5. OPULENT   E. Having or showing great wealth
B - 6. DEMURRED   F. To be discontented or low in spirits
Y - 7. QUIESCENT   G. Inactive; not working; being lazy
H - 8. IMPORTUNING   H. Persistently pleading
J - 9. LOATH   I. Ate
P - 10. LANGUOR   J. Reluctant
L - 11. PURGED   K. Emotionally upset
Q - 12. PITEOUS   L. Purified; rid of undesirable elements
C - 13. AGAPE   M. Slick; characterized by insincere earnestness
I - 14. SUPPED   N. Devised; planned; managed
W - 15. REAPED   O. Making less of something
D - 16. FRUGAL   P. Lack of energy; listlessness
K - 17. DISTRAUGHT   Q. Deserving pity
O - 18. DEPRECIATION   R. Twist; squirm; contort
R - 19. WRITHE   S. Characterized by fluent speech
U - 20. PEEVISHLY   T. Like a slave
M - 21. UNCTUOUS   U. In a contrary way
S - 22. VOLUBLY   V. Tarried; loitered; also means flirted
A - 23. MUSING   W. Harvested; cut and collected
F - 24. REPINE   X. Forced
X - 25. COMPELLED   Y. Quiet; still; inactive

Good Earth Vocabulary Matching 2

1. DISTRAUGHT — A. Withered; wrinkled
2. PURGED — B. Continuous
3. QUIESCENT — C. Deserving pity
4. IMPUDENT — D. Full of strength and energy
5. COWERING — E. Cringing in fear
6. INCESSANT — F. State of paralyzing dismay
7. ARDUOUS — G. Harvested; cut and collected
8. DAIS — H. Position of superiority
9. RICKSHA — I. Purified; rid of undesirable elements
10. REAPED — J. Loudly; without restraint
11. OPULENT — K. Devised; planned; managed
12. SCRUPULOUS — L. To long for; to have feelings of tenderness for
13. BLEARY — M. Having or showing great wealth
14. QUERULOUSLY — N. Quiet; still; inactive
15. MUSING — O. Blurred and/or reddened
16. PITEOUS — P. Objected
17. CONTRIVED — Q. Grumblingly; complainingly
18. ROBUST — R. Gruff
19. CONSTERNATION — S. Raised platform
20. BOISTEROUSLY — T. Small, two-wheeled carriage pulled by 1 or 2 people
21. YEARN — U. Considering thoughtfully
22. DEMURRED — V. Emotionally upset
23. EMINENCE — W. Conscientious; exact
24. SURLY — X. Bold and offensive
25. WIZENED — Y. Difficult

Good Earth Vocabulary Matching 2 Answer Key

V - 1.	DISTRAUGHT	A.	Withered; wrinkled
I - 2.	PURGED	B.	Continuous
N - 3.	QUIESCENT	C.	Deserving pity
X - 4.	IMPUDENT	D.	Full of strength and energy
E - 5.	COWERING	E.	Cringing in fear
B - 6.	INCESSANT	F.	State of paralyzing dismay
Y - 7.	ARDUOUS	G.	Harvested; cut and collected
S - 8.	DAIS	H.	Position of superiority
T - 9.	RICKSHA	I.	Purified; rid of undesirable elements
G - 10.	REAPED	J.	Loudly; without restraint
M - 11.	OPULENT	K.	Devised; planned; managed
W - 12.	SCRUPULOUS	L.	To long for; to have feelings of tenderness for
O - 13.	BLEARY	M.	Having or showing great wealth
Q - 14.	QUERULOUSLY	N.	Quiet; still; inactive
U - 15.	MUSING	O.	Blurred and/or reddened
C - 16.	PITEOUS	P.	Objected
K - 17.	CONTRIVED	Q.	Grumblingly; complainingly
D - 18.	ROBUST	R.	Gruff
F - 19.	CONSTERNATION	S.	Raised platform
J - 20.	BOISTEROUSLY	T.	Small, two-wheeled carriage pulled by 1 or 2 people
L - 21.	YEARN	U.	Considering thoughtfully
P - 22.	DEMURRED	V.	Emotionally upset
H - 23.	EMINENCE	W.	Conscientious; exact
R - 24.	SURLY	X.	Bold and offensive
A - 25.	WIZENED	Y.	Difficult

Good Earth Vocabulary Matching 3

___ 1. COQUETRY   A. Conscientious; exact
___ 2. DALLIED   B. Twist; squirm; contort
___ 3. UNCTUOUS   C. Withered; wrinkled
___ 4. INCESSANT   D. Purified; rid of undesirable elements
___ 5. ZENITH   E. Tarried; loitered; also means flirted
___ 6. PITEOUS   F. Like a slave
___ 7. DEMURRED   G. Gave reluctantly or resentfully
___ 8. SHREWISH   H. Slick; characterized by insincere earnestness
___ 9. COMPELLED   I. Gestures of homage, deference, or reverence
___10. REPINE   J. Grumblingly; complainingly
___11. OPULENT   K. Showing moral excellence, virtue, or chastity
___12. WIZENED   L. Flirting
___13. SLAVISHLY   M. Unshakable; calm and steady
___14. BEGRUDGED   N. Highest point
___15. OBEISANCES   O. Ill-humored
___16. IMPORTUNING   P. Passively agreeable
___17. QUERULOUSLY   Q. Objected
___18. IMPERTURBABLE   R. Continuous
___19. ACQUIESCENT   S. Persistently pleading
___20. SCRUPULOUS   T. Deserving pity
___21. BLEARY   U. Blurred and/or reddened
___22. WRITHE   V. Devised; planned; managed
___23. CONTRIVED   W. Forced
___24. PURGED   X. To be discontented or low in spirits
___25. VIRTUOUSLY   Y. Having or showing great wealth

Good Earth Vocabulary Matching 3 Answer Key

L - 1.	COQUETRY	A. Conscientious; exact
E - 2.	DALLIED	B. Twist; squirm; contort
H - 3.	UNCTUOUS	C. Withered; wrinkled
R - 4.	INCESSANT	D. Purified; rid of undesirable elements
N - 5.	ZENITH	E. Tarried; loitered; also means flirted
T - 6.	PITEOUS	F. Like a slave
Q - 7.	DEMURRED	G. Gave reluctantly or resentfully
O - 8.	SHREWISH	H. Slick; characterized by insincere earnestness
W - 9.	COMPELLED	I. Gestures of homage, deference, or reverence
X -10.	REPINE	J. Grumblingly; complainingly
Y -11.	OPULENT	K. Showing moral excellence, virtue, or chastity
C -12.	WIZENED	L. Flirting
F -13.	SLAVISHLY	M. Unshakable; calm and steady
G -14.	BEGRUDGED	N. Highest point
I -15.	OBEISANCES	O. Ill-humored
S -16.	IMPORTUNING	P. Passively agreeable
J -17.	QUERULOUSLY	Q. Objected
M -18.	IMPERTURBABLE	R. Continuous
P -19.	ACQUIESCENT	S. Persistently pleading
A -20.	SCRUPULOUS	T. Deserving pity
U -21.	BLEARY	U. Blurred and/or reddened
B -22.	WRITHE	V. Devised; planned; managed
V -23.	CONTRIVED	W. Forced
D -24.	PURGED	X. To be discontented or low in spirits
K -25.	VIRTUOUSLY	Y. Having or showing great wealth

Good Earth Vocabulary Matching 4

___ 1. IMPORTUNING A. To be discontented or low in spirits
___ 2. PURGED B. Characterized by fluent speech
___ 3. PAGODA C. Cringing in fear
___ 4. OBEISANCES D. Purified; rid of undesirable elements
___ 5. DISTRAUGHT E. Having or showing great wealth
___ 6. PETULANT F. Full of strength and energy
___ 7. OPULENT G. Clothed
___ 8. IDLE H. Gestures of homage, deference, or reverence
___ 9. CLAD I. To long for; to have feelings of tenderness for
___10. DAIS J. Unshakable; calm and steady
___11. YEARN K. Raised platform
___12. VOLUBLY L. Twist; squirm; contort
___13. IMPUDENT M. Devised; planned; managed
___14. ARDUOUS N. Emotionally upset
___15. DEPRECIATION O. Quiet; still; inactive
___16. SLAVISHLY P. Unreasonably ill-tempered
___17. COWERING Q. Ill-humored
___18. IMPERTURBABLE R. Multi-story Buddhist tower
___19. REPINE S. Inactive; not working; being lazy
___20. ROBUST T. Bold and offensive
___21. SHREWISH U. Difficult
___22. CONTRIVED V. Making less of something
___23. WRITHE W. In a state of wonder or amazement
___24. QUIESCENT X. Like a slave
___25. AGAPE Y. Persistently pleading

Good Earth Vocabulary Matching 4 Answer Key

Y - 1. IMPORTUNING	A.	To be discontented or low in spirits
D - 2. PURGED	B.	Characterized by fluent speech
R - 3. PAGODA	C.	Cringing in fear
H - 4. OBEISANCES	D.	Purified; rid of undesirable elements
N - 5. DISTRAUGHT	E.	Having or showing great wealth
P - 6. PETULANT	F.	Full of strength and energy
E - 7. OPULENT	G.	Clothed
S - 8. IDLE	H.	Gestures of homage, deference, or reverence
G - 9. CLAD	I.	To long for; to have feelings of tenderness for
K - 10. DAIS	J.	Unshakable; calm and steady
I - 11. YEARN	K.	Raised platform
B - 12. VOLUBLY	L.	Twist; squirm; contort
T - 13. IMPUDENT	M.	Devised; planned; managed
U - 14. ARDUOUS	N.	Emotionally upset
V - 15. DEPRECIATION	O.	Quiet; still; inactive
X - 16. SLAVISHLY	P.	Unreasonably ill-tempered
C - 17. COWERING	Q.	Ill-humored
J - 18. IMPERTURBABLE	R.	Multi-story Buddhist tower
A - 19. REPINE	S.	Inactive; not working; being lazy
F - 20. ROBUST	T.	Bold and offensive
Q - 21. SHREWISH	U.	Difficult
M - 22. CONTRIVED	V.	Making less of something
L - 23. WRITHE	W.	In a state of wonder or amazement
O - 24. QUIESCENT	X.	Like a slave
W - 25. AGAPE	Y.	Persistently pleading

Good Earth Vocabulary Magic Squares 1

Match the definition with the vocabulary word. Put your answers in the magic squares below. When your answers are correct, all columns and rows will add to the same number.

A. ARDUOUS
B. RICKSHA
C. QUIESCENT
D. AGAPE
E. ROBUST
F. CONSTERNATION

G. EMINENCE
H. PAGODA
I. VOLUBLY
J. PITEOUS
K. REMORSE
L. CLAD

M. PETULANT
N. CONCUBINES
O. IDLE
P. SHREWISH

1. Inactive; not working; being lazy
2. In a state of wonder or amazement
3. Deserving pity
4. Full of strength and energy
5. Characterized by fluent speech
6. State of paralyzing dismay
7. Ill-humored
8. Quiet; still; inactive
9. Multi-story Buddhist tower
10. Bitter regret
11. Difficult
12. Women contracted as second wives
13. Small, two-wheeled carriage pulled by 1 or 2 people
14. Unreasonably ill-tempered
15. Position of superiority
16. Clothed

A=	B=	C=	D=
E=	F=	G=	H=
I=	J=	K=	L=
M=	N=	O=	P=

Good Earth Vocabulary Magic Squares 1 Answer Key

Match the definition with the vocabulary word. Put your answers in the magic squares below. When your answers are correct, all columns and rows will add to the same number.

A. ARDUOUS
B. RICKSHA
C. QUIESCENT
D. AGAPE
E. ROBUST
F. CONSTERNATION
G. EMINENCE
H. PAGODA
I. VOLUBLY
J. PITEOUS
K. REMORSE
L. CLAD
M. PETULANT
N. CONCUBINES
O. IDLE
P. SHREWISH

1. Inactive; not working; being lazy
2. In a state of wonder or amazement
3. Deserving pity
4. Full of strength and energy
5. Characterized by fluent speech
6. State of paralyzing dismay
7. Ill-humored
8. Quiet; still; inactive
9. Multi-story Buddhist tower
10. Bitter regret
11. Difficult
12. Women contracted as second wives
13. Small, two-wheeled carriage pulled by 1 or 2 people
14. Unreasonably ill-tempered
15. Position of superiority
16. Clothed

A=11	B=13	C=8	D=2
E=4	F=6	G=15	H=9
I=5	J=3	K=10	L=16
M=14	N=12	O=1	P=7

Good Earth Vocabulary Magic Squares 2

Match the definition with the vocabulary word. Put your answers in the magic squares below. When your answers are correct, all columns and rows will add to the same number.

A. BEGRUDGED
B. QUIESCENT
C. IDLE
D. WIZENED
E. MUSING
F. ARDENT
G. SUPPED
H. LOWED
I. BLEARY
J. PURGED
K. VIRTUOUSLY
L. CONCUBINES
M. INCESSANT
N. SLAVISHLY
O. YEARN
P. WRITHE

1. Continuous
2. Passionate; full of strong feeling or enthusiasm
3. Mooed
4. To long for; to have feelings of tenderness for
5. Women contracted as second wives
6. Inactive; not working; being lazy
7. Gave reluctantly or resentfully
8. Purified; rid of undesirable elements
9. Showing moral excellence, virtue, or chastity
10. Withered; wrinkled
11. Quiet; still; inactive
12. Blurred and/or reddened
13. Like a slave
14. Considering thoughtfully
15. Ate
16. Twist; squirm; contort

A=	B=	C=	D=
E=	F=	G=	H=
I=	J=	K=	L=
M=	N=	O=	P=

Good Earth Vocabulary Magic Squares 2 Answer Key

Match the definition with the vocabulary word. Put your answers in the magic squares below. When your answers are correct, all columns and rows will add to the same number.

A. BEGRUDGED
B. QUIESCENT
C. IDLE
D. WIZENED
E. MUSING
F. ARDENT
G. SUPPED
H. LOWED
I. BLEARY
J. PURGED
K. VIRTUOUSLY
L. CONCUBINES
M. INCESSANT
N. SLAVISHLY
O. YEARN
P. WRITHE

1. Continuous
2. Passionate; full of strong feeling or enthusiasm
3. Mooed
4. To long for; to have feelings of tenderness for
5. Women contracted as second wives
6. Inactive; not working; being lazy
7. Gave reluctantly or resentfully
8. Purified; rid of undesirable elements
9. Showing moral excellence, virtue, or chastity
10. Withered; wrinkled
11. Quiet; still; inactive
12. Blurred and/or reddened
13. Like a slave
14. Considering thoughtfully
15. Ate
16. Twist; squirm; contort

A=7	B=11	C=6	D=10
E=14	F=2	G=15	H=3
I=12	J=8	K=9	L=5
M=1	N=13	O=4	P=16

Good Earth Vocabulary Magic Squares 3

Match the definition with the vocabulary word. Put your answers in the magic squares below. When your answers are correct, all columns and rows will add to the same number.

A. SURLY
B. COQUETRY
C. FRUGAL
D. PETULANT
E. PEEVISHLY
F. ROBUST
G. PURGED
H. YEARN
I. IDLE
J. BEGRUDGED
K. REAPED
L. DEMURRED
M. DAIS
N. SLAVISHLY
O. WIZENED
P. BERATE

1. Flirting
2. Purified; rid of undesirable elements
3. Harvested; cut and collected
4. Like a slave
5. Raised platform
6. Objected
7. To long for; to have feelings of tenderness for
8. Gruff
9. Reprimand; scold
10. Inactive; not working; being lazy
11. In a contrary way
12. Unreasonably ill-tempered
13. Thrifty; tight with money
14. Full of strength and energy
15. Gave reluctantly or resentfully
16. Withered; wrinkled

A=	B=	C=	D=
E=	F=	G=	H=
I=	J=	K=	L=
M=	N=	O=	P=

Good Earth Vocabulary Magic Squares 3 Answer Key

Match the definition with the vocabulary word. Put your answers in the magic squares below. When your answers are correct, all columns and rows will add to the same number.

A. SURLY
B. COQUETRY
C. FRUGAL
D. PETULANT
E. PEEVISHLY
F. ROBUST
G. PURGED
H. YEARN
I. IDLE
J. BEGRUDGED
K. REAPED
L. DEMURRED
M. DAIS
N. SLAVISHLY
O. WIZENED
P. BERATE

1. Flirting
2. Purified; rid of undesirable elements
3. Harvested; cut and collected
4. Like a slave
5. Raised platform
6. Objected
7. To long for; to have feelings of tenderness for
8. Gruff
9. Reprimand; scold
10. Inactive; not working; being lazy
11. In a contrary way
12. Unreasonably ill-tempered
13. Thrifty; tight with money
14. Full of strength and energy
15. Gave reluctantly or resentfully
16. Withered; wrinkled

A=8	B=1	C=13	D=12
E=11	F=14	G=2	H=7
I=10	J=15	K=3	L=6
M=5	N=4	O=16	P=9

Good Earth Vocabulary Magic Squares 4

Match the definition with the vocabulary word. Put your answers in the magic squares below. When your answers are correct, all columns and rows will add to the same number.

A. LOATH
B. AGAPE
C. BERATE
D. IMPORTUNING
E. PITEOUS
F. SHREWISH
G. DISTRAUGHT
H. COWERING
I. ROBUST
J. CONSTERNATION
K. BEGRUDGED
L. LOWED
M. MALICE
N. FRUGAL
O. VOLUBLY
P. ARDENT

1. Reluctant
2. Thrifty; tight with money
3. State of paralyzing dismay
4. Deserving pity
5. Emotionally upset
6. Mooed
7. Passionate; full of strong feeling or enthusiasm
8. Reprimand; scold
9. Characterized by fluent speech
10. Persistently pleading
11. Cringing in fear
12. Gave reluctantly or resentfully
13. Full of strength and energy
14. Ill-humored
15. In a state of wonder or amazement
16. Intent of ill-will

A=	B=	C=	D=
E=	F=	G=	H=
I=	J=	K=	L=
M=	N=	O=	P=

85
Copyrighted

Good Earth Vocabulary Magic Squares 4 Answer Key

Match the definition with the vocabulary word. Put your answers in the magic squares below. When your answers are correct, all columns and rows will add to the same number.

A. LOATH
B. AGAPE
C. BERATE
D. IMPORTUNING
E. PITEOUS
F. SHREWISH
G. DISTRAUGHT
H. COWERING
I. ROBUST
J. CONSTERNATION
K. BEGRUDGED
L. LOWED
M. MALICE
N. FRUGAL
O. VOLUBLY
P. ARDENT

1. Reluctant
2. Thrifty; tight with money
3. State of paralyzing dismay
4. Deserving pity
5. Emotionally upset
6. Mooed
7. Passionate; full of strong feeling or enthusiasm
8. Reprimand; scold
9. Characterized by fluent speech
10. Persistently pleading
11. Cringing in fear
12. Gave reluctantly or resentfully
13. Full of strength and energy
14. Ill-humored
15. In a state of wonder or amazement
16. Intent of ill-will

A=1	B=15	C=8	D=10
E=4	F=14	G=5	H=11
I=13	J=3	K=12	L=6
M=16	N=2	O=9	P=7

Good Earth Vocabulary Word Search 1

Words are placed backwards, forward, diagonally, up and down. Clues listed below can help you find the words. Circle the hidden vocabulary words in the maze.

```
C O N T R I V E D N Z R E A P E D F
B D W M H A R D U O U S N G E S G Y
E Q R W E M I N E N C E L G E H V Z
R D S Q L P P U R G E D Q T V R Z J
A I B C B P A G O D A A Z S I E L Y
T S D Y A S X L R N H L E U S W O Z
E T D C B T A D E D P L N B H I A Z
S R L Q R G M V M T S I I O L S T T
L A N G U O R C O Q U E T R Y H H J
D U R R T E O W R L O D H E Y K G S
Q G F D R W C S M U X V X O M N N
S H R K E T Q U E C T B D K C U I L
T T L R P N W S L P C Y L R U S S B
L F I I M E T I M O N B E Y U J U P
L N D C I D Q A Z L U P L O H M M L
G F Z K M U I D L E I S L E P A G A
Y K P S X P D E W N N U L N A M M D
S E H H D M P W E R P E Y Y D R E B
Y S A A L I L O T U I D D T K P Y M
F B P R L P Y L R L C T Z Q P R T L
V S F R N S E C I L A M H U S B V B
F T T K N G S H T N A S S E C N I T
```

Ate (6)
Bitter regret (7)
Blurred and/or reddened (6)
Bold and offensive (8)
Characterized by fluent speech (7)
Clothed (4)
Conscientious; exact (10)
Considering thoughtfully (6)
Continuous (9)
Cringing in fear (8)
Deserving pity (7)
Devised; planned; managed (9)
Difficult (7)
Emotionally upset (10)
Flirting (8)
Full of strength and energy (6)
Gruff (5)
Grumblingly; complainingly (11)
Harvested; cut and collected (6)
Highest point (6)
Ill-humored (8)
In a contrary way (9)
In a state of wonder or amazement (5)

Inactive; not working; being lazy (4)
Intent of ill-will (6)
Lack of energy; listlessness (7)
Mooed (5)
Multi-story Buddhist tower (6)
Passionate; full of strong feeling or enthusiasm (6)
Position of superiority (8)
Purified; rid of undesirable elements (6)
Raised platform (4)
Reluctant (5)
Reprimand; scold (6)
Slick; characterized by insincere earnestness (8)
Small, two-wheeled carriage pulled by 1 or 2 people (7)
Tarried; loitered; also means flirted (7)
Thrifty; tight with money (6)
To be discontented or low in spirits (6)
To long for; to have feelings of tenderness for (5)
Twist; squirm; contort (6)
Unshakable; calm and steady (13)
Withered; wrinkled (7)

Good Earth Vocabulary Word Search 1 Answer Key

Words are placed backwards, forward, diagonally, up and down. Clues listed below can help you find the words. Circle the hidden vocabulary words in the maze.

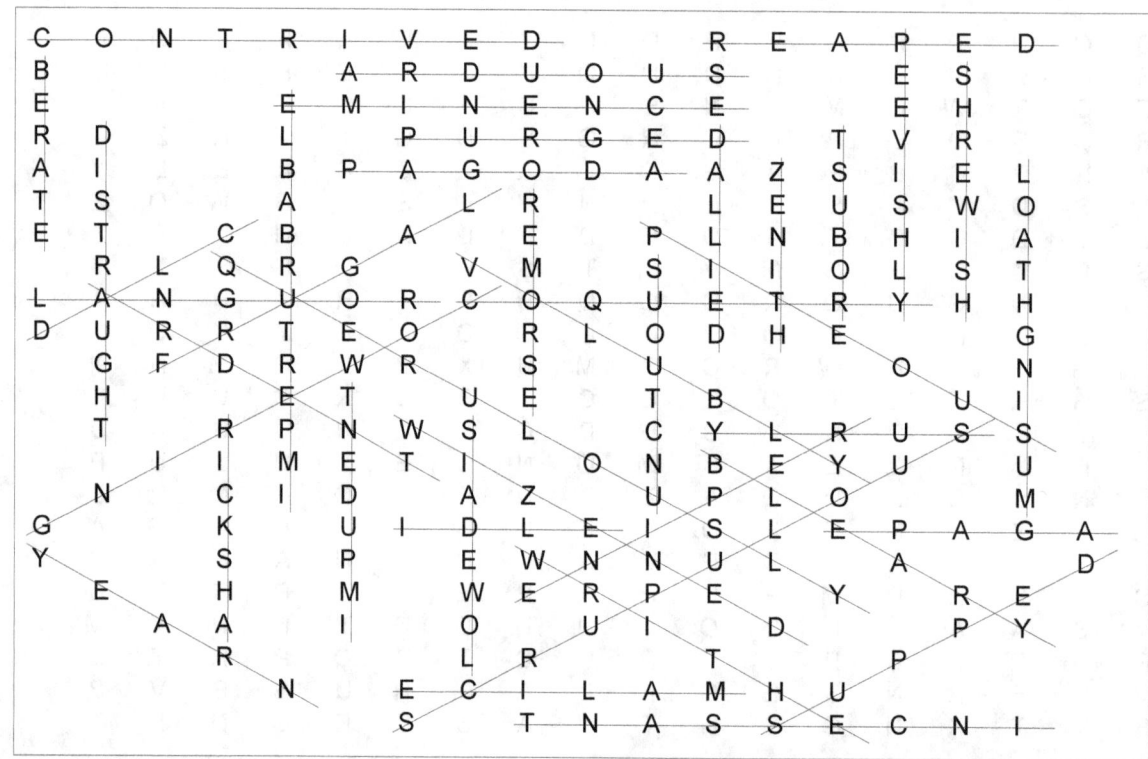

Ate (6)
Bitter regret (7)
Blurred and/or reddened (6)
Bold and offensive (8)
Characterized by fluent speech (7)
Clothed (4)
Conscientious; exact (10)
Considering thoughtfully (6)
Continuous (9)
Cringing in fear (8)
Deserving pity (7)
Devised; planned; managed (9)
Difficult (7)
Emotionally upset (10)
Flirting (8)
Full of strength and energy (6)
Gruff (5)
Grumblingly; complainingly (11)
Harvested; cut and collected (6)
Highest point (6)
Ill-humored (8)
In a contrary way (9)
In a state of wonder or amazement (5)

Inactive; not working; being lazy (4)
Intent of ill-will (6)
Lack of energy; listlessness (7)
Mooed (5)
Multi-story Buddhist tower (6)
Passionate; full of strong feeling or enthusiasm (6)
Position of superiority (8)
Purified; rid of undesirable elements (6)
Raised platform (4)
Reluctant (5)
Reprimand; scold (6)
Slick; characterized by insincere earnestness (8)
Small, two-wheeled carriage pulled by 1 or 2 people (7)
Tarried; loitered; also means flirted (7)
Thrifty; tight with money (6)
To be discontented or low in spirits (6)
To long for; to have feelings of tenderness for (5)
Twist; squirm; contort (6)
Unshakable; calm and steady (13)
Withered; wrinkled (7)

Good Earth Vocabulary Word Search 2

Words are placed backwards, forward, diagonally, up and down. Clues listed below can help you find the words. Circle the hidden vocabulary words in the maze.

```
V I R T U O U S L Y C L A G A P E Y
V O L U B L Y H U B T G O Y T R R Z
S U P P E D Z R L R W C K W P G O G
H D E M U R R E D O L Z H Q E K B S
R I C K S H A W Q F A Y Y U T D U W
D C O Q L R C I S R W T L I U D S X
E O N R Y N W S Z U D T H E L E T L
P N S S J V F H I G S N S S A V M X
R C T Y L B B K N A V T I C N I L R
E U E J P A D C C L K N V E T R A Q
C B R F F W V D E G G E E N X T N J
I I N H B M S I S E P L E T S N G F
A N A R D U O U S C R U P U L O U S
T E T L E S S R A H F P R K N C O T
I S I W M M O P N L L O W G B S R L
O K O Z G M I B T T K Y A E E N P K
N G N R E P I N E H T I R W R D I Z
S K B R C N A L E F F A D A E A T W
K L W V I G I G R N T S E B A I E K
D E I L L A D T O E C Y N G P S O J
S G P M A T V D H D P E T B E V U K
I D L E M U S I N G A C L A D N S C
```

Ate (6)
Bitter regret (7)
Blurred and/or reddened (6)
Characterized by fluent speech (7)
Clothed (4)
Conscientious; exact (10)
Considering thoughtfully (6)
Continuous (9)
Deserving pity (7)
Devised; planned; managed (9)
Difficult (7)
Full of strength and energy (6)
Gruff (5)
Harvested; cut and collected (6)
Having or showing great wealth (7)
Highest point (6)
Ill-humored (8)
In a contrary way (9)
In a state of wonder or amazement (5)
Inactive; not working; being lazy (4)
Intent of ill-will (6)
Lack of energy; listlessness (7)
Like a slave (9)
Making less of something (12)
Mooed (5)
Multi-story Buddhist tower (6)
Objected (8)
Passionate; full of strong feeling or enthusiasm (6)
Position of superiority (8)
Purified; rid of undesirable elements (6)
Quiet; still; inactive (9)
Raised platform (4)
Reluctant (5)
Reprimand; scold (6)
Showing moral excellence, virtue, or chastity (10)
Small, two-wheeled carriage pulled by 1 or 2 people (7)
State of paralyzing dismay (13)
Tarried; loitered; also means flirted (7)
Thrifty; tight with money (6)
To be discontented or low in spirits (6)
To long for; to have feelings of tenderness for (5)
Twist; squirm; contort (6)
Unreasonably ill-tempered (8)
Women contracted as second wives (10)

Good Earth Vocabulary Word Search 2 Answer Key

Words are placed backwards, forward, diagonally, up and down. Clues listed below can help you find the words. Circle the hidden vocabulary words in the maze.

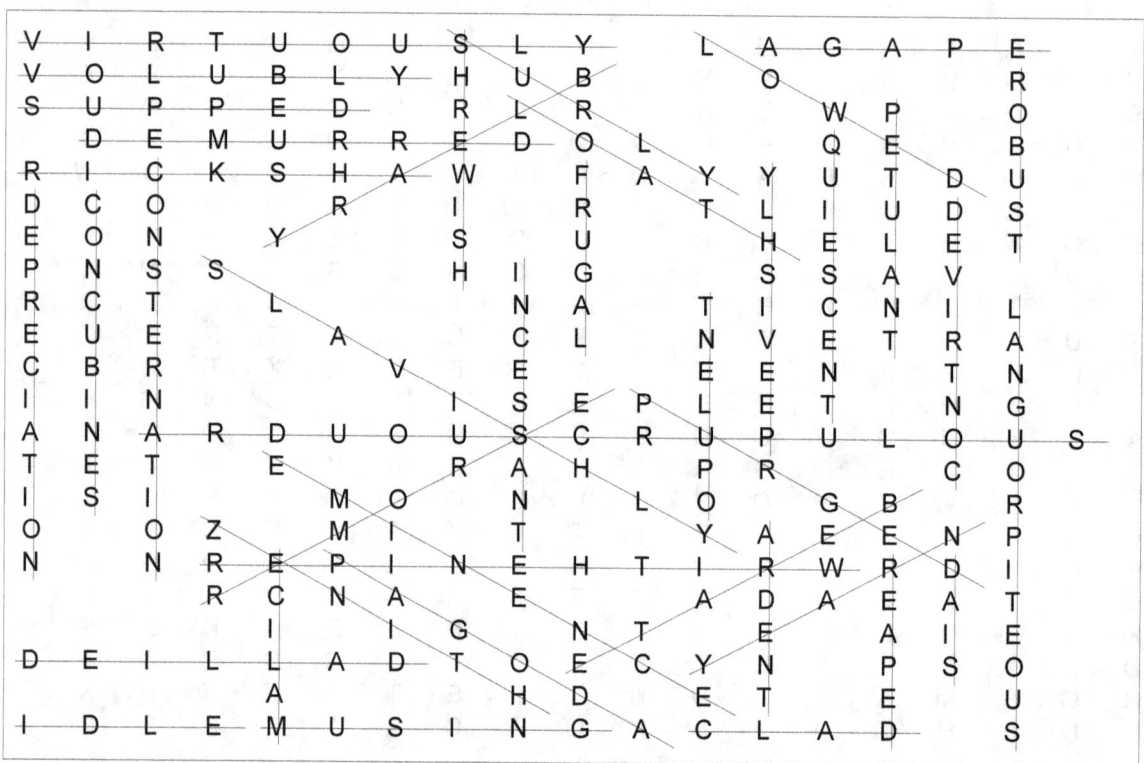

Ate (6)
Bitter regret (7)
Blurred and/or reddened (6)
Characterized by fluent speech (7)
Clothed (4)
Conscientious; exact (10)
Considering thoughtfully (6)
Continuous (9)
Deserving pity (7)
Devised; planned; managed (9)
Difficult (7)
Full of strength and energy (6)
Gruff (5)
Harvested; cut and collected (6)
Having or showing great wealth (7)
Highest point (6)
Ill-humored (8)
In a contrary way (9)
In a state of wonder or amazement (5)
Inactive; not working; being lazy (4)
Intent of ill-will (6)
Lack of energy; listlessness (7)
Like a slave (9)

Making less of something (12)
Mooed (5)
Multi-story Buddhist tower (6)
Objected (8)
Passionate; full of strong feeling or enthusiasm (6)
Position of superiority (8)
Purified; rid of undesirable elements (6)
Quiet; still; inactive (9)
Raised platform (4)
Reluctant (5)
Reprimand; scold (6)
Showing moral excellence, virtue, or chastity (10)
Small, two-wheeled carriage pulled by 1 or 2 people (7)
State of paralyzing dismay (13)
Tarried; loitered; also means flirted (7)
Thrifty; tight with money (6)
To be discontented or low in spirits (6)
To long for; to have feelings of tenderness for (5)
Twist; squirm; contort (6)
Unreasonably ill-tempered (8)
Women contracted as second wives (10)

Good Earth Vocabulary Word Search 3

Words are placed backwards, forward, diagonally, up and down. Words listed below are included in the maze. Circle the hidden vocabulary words in the maze.

```
Q F R U G A L S H R E W I S H Z E V
U J N L H X U L N C M I I U B N S V
E B W T T O H A M O I M N P I M R T
R C A N U W C V U W N P C P D A O D
U O P T C R S I S E E E E E L L M D
L C C D L I D S I R R S D E I E V
O C O G A T A H N I C T S Y B C R F
U Z N N D H L G N E U A D F E E H
S E T K S E L Y D G R R N P A P V W
L N R L N T I P X L X B T S A I H F
Y I I P O D E X Y L F A Y G S G S T
I T V D S W D R B R B A U R G L J
M H E E U C E C N I X L O O N S A Y
P Q D M O M G D C A T E B P W Y N V
U B V U U B X K Z Z T U M U D E G R
D T E R D X S J W I S I Q L G A U B
E V R R R H H G P T H T O E T R O Y
N N E E A C Q U I E S C E N T N R C
T H A D H T R C J C Y L E T V A K R
W G P N D G E P A G O D A F E S N Q
M D E N E Z I W L M R V O L U B L Y
Q G D D P E T U L A N T B L K F M L
```

ACQUIESCENT	DEMURRED	OPULENT	SHREWISH
AGAPE	EMINENCE	PAGODA	SLAVISHLY
ARDENT	FRUGAL	PETULANT	SUPPED
ARDUOUS	IDLE	PITEOUS	SURLY
BERATE	IMPERTURBABLE	PURGED	UNCTUOUS
BLEARY	IMPUDENT	QUERULOUSLY	VOLUBLY
CLAD	INCESSANT	QUIESCENT	WIZENED
CONSTERNATION	LANGUOR	REAPED	WRITHE
CONTRIVED	LOATH	REMORSE	YEARN
COWERING	LOWED	REPINE	ZENITH
DAIS	MALICE	RICKSHA	
DALLIED	MUSING	ROBUST	

Good Earth Vocabulary Word Search 3 Answer Key

Words are placed backwards, forward, diagonally, up and down. Words listed below are included in the maze. Circle the hidden vocabulary words in the maze.

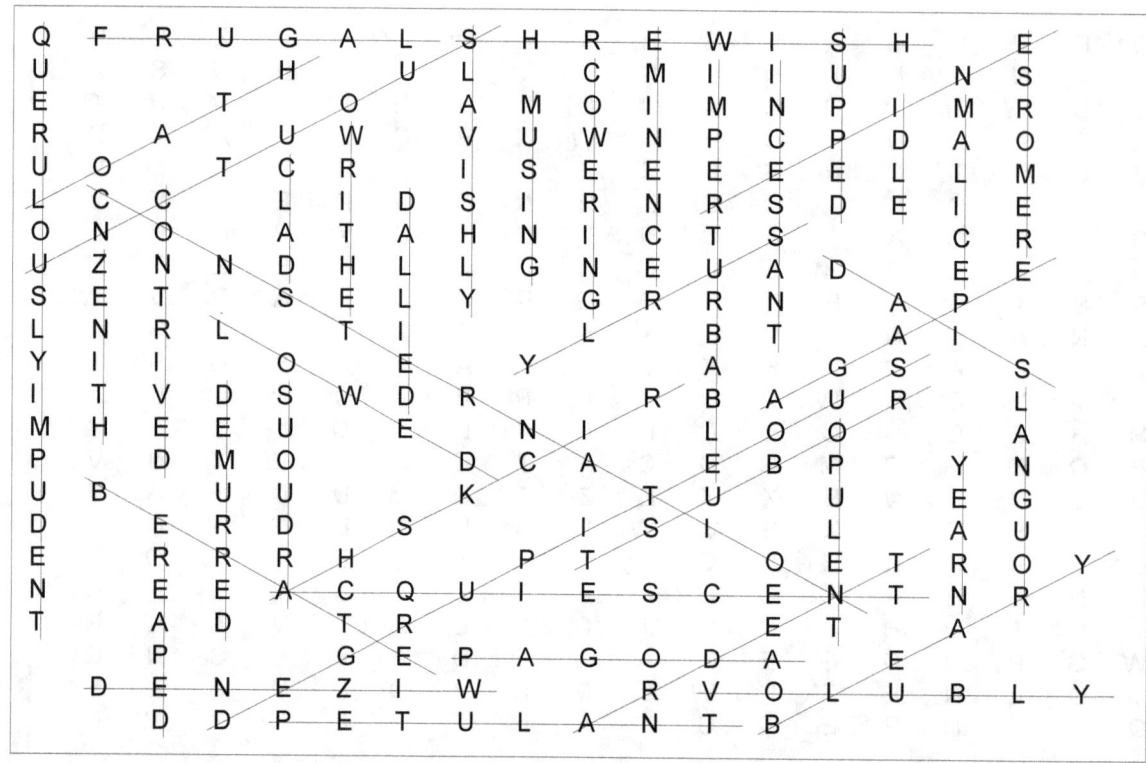

ACQUIESCENT	DEMURRED	OPULENT	SHREWISH
AGAPE	EMINENCE	PAGODA	SLAVISHLY
ARDENT	FRUGAL	PETULANT	SUPPED
ARDUOUS	IDLE	PITEOUS	SURLY
BERATE	IMPERTURBABLE	PURGED	UNCTUOUS
BLEARY	IMPUDENT	QUERULOUSLY	VOLUBLY
CLAD	INCESSANT	QUIESCENT	WIZENED
CONSTERNATION	LANGUOR	REAPED	WRITHE
CONTRIVED	LOATH	REMORSE	YEARN
COWERING	LOWED	REPINE	ZENITH
DAIS	MALICE	RICKSHA	
DALLIED	MUSING	ROBUST	

Good Earth Vocabulary Word Search 4

Words are placed backwards, forward, diagonally, up and down. Words listed below are included in the maze. Circle the hidden vocabulary words in the maze.

```
C O N T R I V E D I N C E S S A N T
O Y L H S I V A L S H L U M V O Z N
W L A G U R F H J S L O V D I B K J
E J M U S I N G F C U W J C R E G S
R T N A L U T E P T Q H L V T I O V
I N Z R D R W X C D T M A O U S P Q
N E E T E X E N Z A A E N L O A U H
G D N S M Q U P O L N P G U U N L J
M U I I U V E L I C S A U B S C E R
I P T D R S M C Z N L G O L L E N S
I M H N R A E Y B L E A R Y Y S T K
M I P O E V L A K J R I D O I C A Q
P P M E D H D X W D C Q H A B R P C
O E S G R O I M U K B S D E D U H N
R E U K G T H O S E U P T E A P S J
T V P A L Q U H G O X A N R L U I T
U I P P W S A R E R R T S E L L W L
N S E U N R U T B E N X U A I O E N
I H D R J D I J B A X B R P E U R Y
N L J G G P S T Q W B N L E D S H Q
G Y F E C F M Z H J S L Y D Y D S J
L V D D L O W E D E J D E N E Z I W
```

AGAPE	DISTRAUGHT	OBEISANCES	SCRUPULOUS
ARDENT	FRUGAL	OPULENT	SHREWISH
ARDUOUS	IDLE	PAGODA	SLAVISHLY
BEGRUDGED	IMPERTURBABLE	PEEVISHLY	SUPPED
BERATE	IMPORTUNING	PETULANT	SURLY
BLEARY	IMPUDENT	PITEOUS	UNCTUOUS
CLAD	INCESSANT	PURGED	VIRTUOUSLY
CONTRIVED	LANGUOR	REAPED	VOLUBLY
COWERING	LOATH	REMORSE	WIZENED
DAIS	LOWED	REPINE	WRITHE
DALLIED	MALICE	RICKSHA	YEARN
DEMURRED	MUSING	ROBUST	ZENITH

Good Earth Vocabulary Word Search 4 Answer Key

Words are placed backwards, forward, diagonally, up and down. Words listed below are included in the maze. Circle the hidden vocabulary words in the maze.

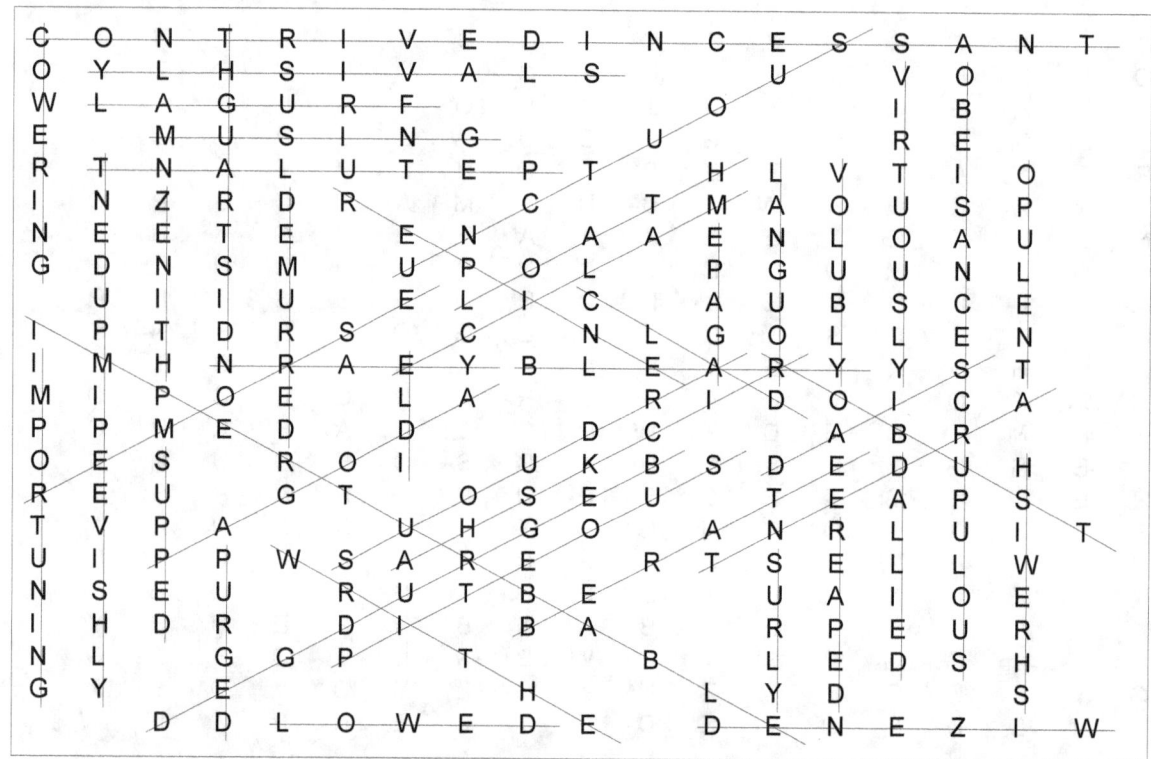

AGAPE	DISTRAUGHT	OBEISANCES	SCRUPULOUS
ARDENT	FRUGAL	OPULENT	SHREWISH
ARDUOUS	IDLE	PAGODA	SLAVISHLY
BEGRUDGED	IMPERTURBABLE	PEEVISHLY	SUPPED
BERATE	IMPORTUNING	PETULANT	SURLY
BLEARY	IMPUDENT	PITEOUS	UNCTUOUS
CLAD	INCESSANT	PURGED	VIRTUOUSLY
CONTRIVED	LANGUOR	REAPED	VOLUBLY
COWERING	LOATH	REMORSE	WIZENED
DAIS	LOWED	REPINE	WRITHE
DALLIED	MALICE	RICKSHA	YEARN
DEMURRED	MUSING	ROBUST	ZENITH

Good Earth Vocabulary Crossword 1

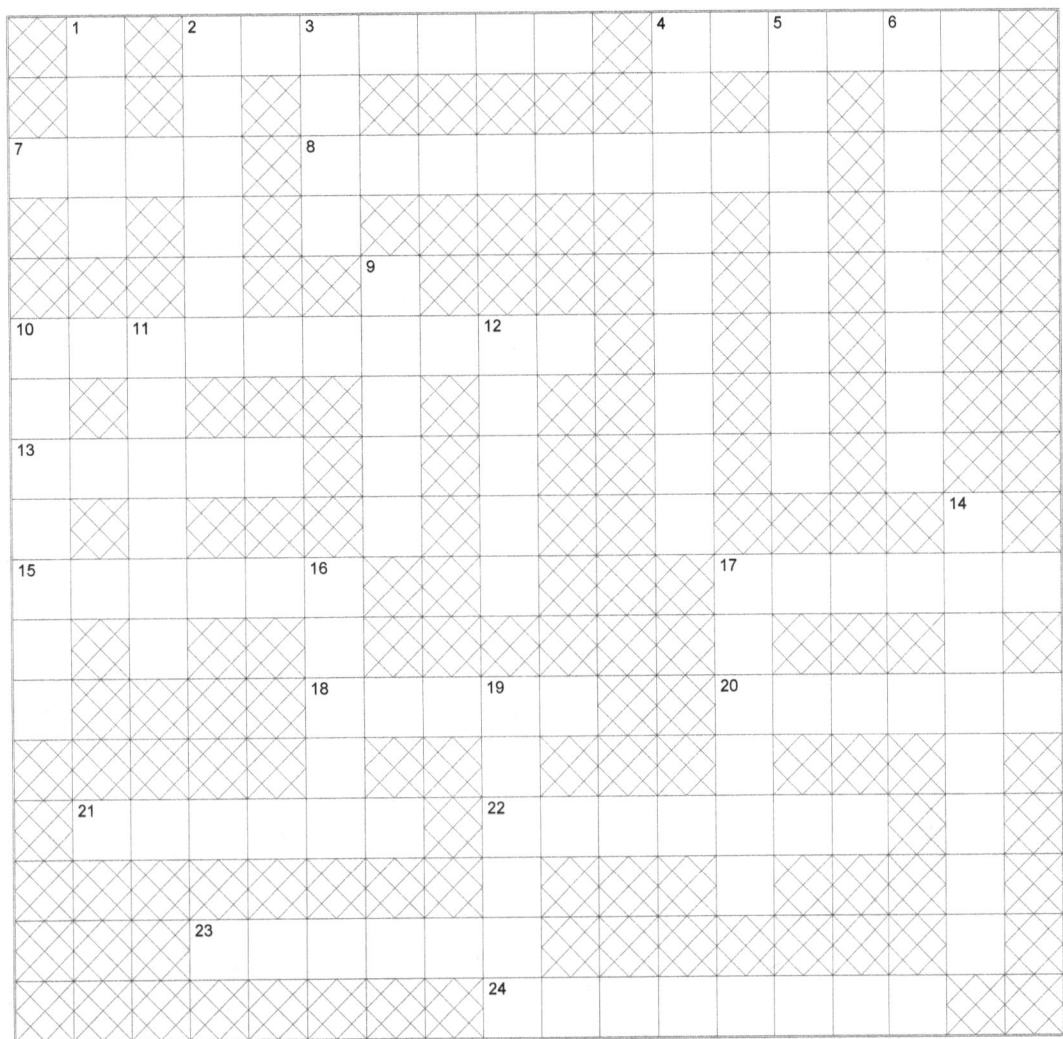

Across
2. Difficult
4. Ate
7. Clothed
8. Continuous
10. Showing moral excellence, virtue, or chastity
13. Reluctant
15. Blurred and/or reddened
17. To be discontented or low in spirits
18. In a state of wonder or amazement
20. Reprimand; scold
21. Considering thoughtfully
22. Small, two-wheeled carriage pulled by 1 or 2 people
23. Twist; squirm; contort
24. Objected

Down
1. Inactive; not working; being lazy
2. Passionate; full of strong feeling or enthusiasm
3. Raised platform
4. Like a slave
5. Unreasonably ill-tempered
6. Position of superiority
9. Gruff
10. Characterized by fluent speech
11. Harvested; cut and collected
12. Mooed
14. Slick; characterized by insincere earnestness
16. To long for; to have feelings of tenderness for
17. Full of strength and energy
19. Purified; rid of undesirable elements

Good Earth Vocabulary Crossword 1 Answer Key

Across
2. Difficult
4. Ate
7. Clothed
8. Continuous
10. Showing moral excellence, virtue, or chastity
13. Reluctant
15. Blurred and/or reddened
17. To be discontented or low in spirits
18. In a state of wonder or amazement
20. Reprimand; scold
21. Considering thoughtfully
22. Small, two-wheeled carriage pulled by 1 or 2 people
23. Twist; squirm; contort
24. Objected

Down
1. Inactive; not working; being lazy
2. Passionate; full of strong feeling or enthusiasm
3. Raised platform
4. Like a slave
5. Unreasonably ill-tempered
6. Position of superiority
9. Gruff
10. Characterized by fluent speech
11. Harvested; cut and collected
12. Mooed
14. Slick; characterized by insincere earnestness
16. To long for; to have feelings of tenderness for
17. Full of strength and energy
19. Purified; rid of undesirable elements

Good Earth Vocabulary Crossword 2

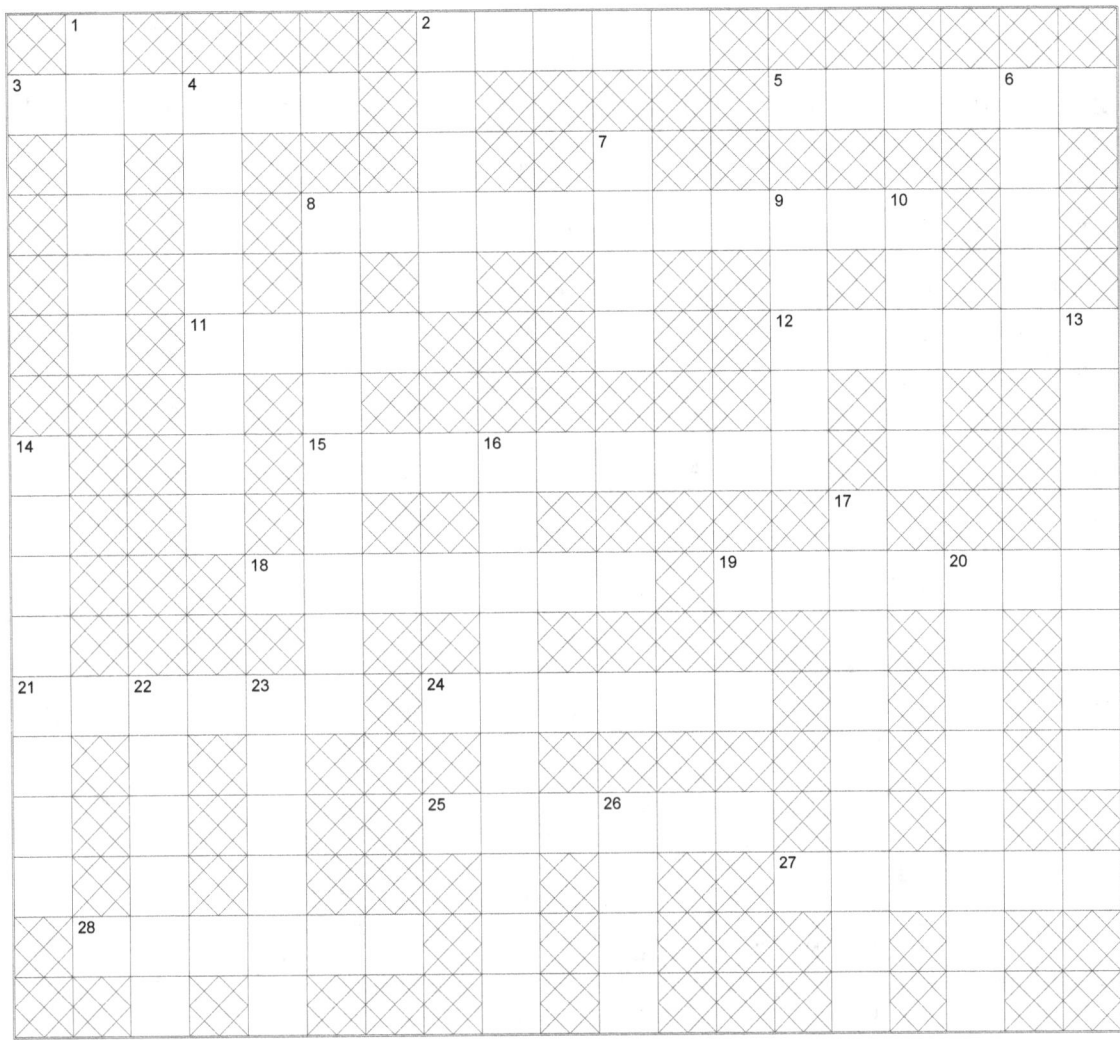

Across
2. Reluctant
3. Highest point
5. Thrifty; tight with money
8. Grumblingly; complainingly
11. Raised platform
12. Harvested; cut and collected
15. Like a slave
18. Bitter regret
19. Lack of energy; listlessness
21. Full of strength and energy
24. Purified; rid of undesirable elements
25. Considering thoughtfully
27. Multi-story Buddhist tower
28. Passionate; full of strong feeling or enthusiasm

Down
1. Reprimand; scold
2. Mooed
4. Bold and offensive
6. In a state of wonder or amazement
7. Clothed
8. Quiet; still; inactive
9. Gruff
10. To long for; to have feelings of tenderness for
13. Objected
14. Cringing in fear
16. Showing moral excellence, virtue, or chastity
17. Continuous
20. Slick; characterized by insincere earnestness
22. Blurred and/or reddened
23. Ate
26. Inactive; not working; being lazy

Good Earth Vocabulary Crossword 2 Answer Key

Across
2. Reluctant
3. Highest point
5. Thrifty; tight with money
8. Grumblingly; complainingly
11. Raised platform
12. Harvested; cut and collected
15. Like a slave
18. Bitter regret
19. Lack of energy; listlessness
21. Full of strength and energy
24. Purified; rid of undesirable elements
25. Considering thoughtfully
27. Multi-story Buddhist tower
28. Passionate; full of strong feeling or enthusiasm

Down
1. Reprimand; scold
2. Mooed
4. Bold and offensive
6. In a state of wonder or amazement
7. Clothed
8. Quiet; still; inactive
9. Gruff
10. To long for; to have feelings of tenderness for
13. Objected
14. Cringing in fear
16. Showing moral excellence, virtue, or chastity
17. Continuous
20. Slick; characterized by insincere earnestness
22. Blurred and/or reddened
23. Ate
26. Inactive; not working; being lazy

Good Earth Vocabulary Crossword 3

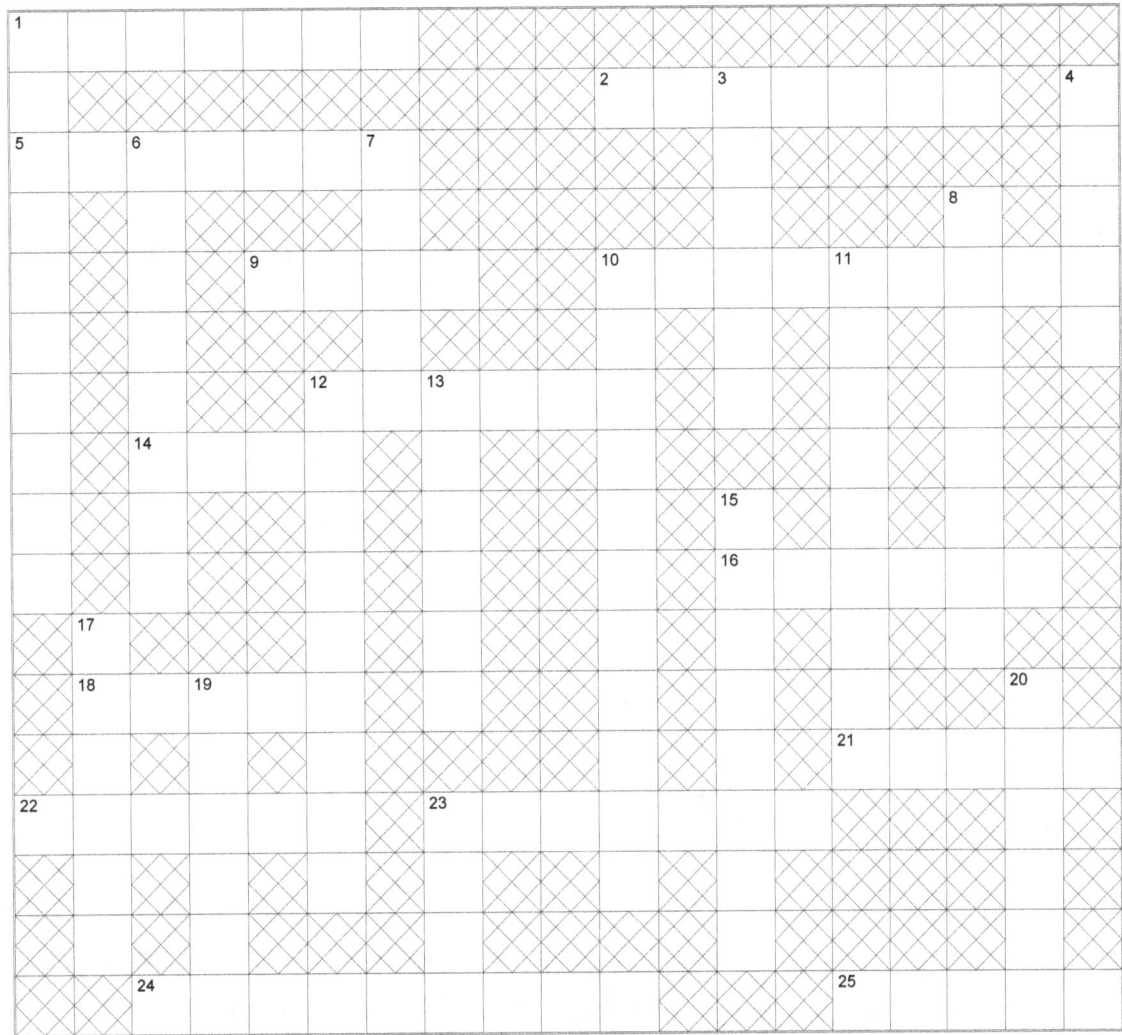

Across
1. Characterized by fluent speech
2. Withered; wrinkled
5. Small, two-wheeled carriage pulled by 1 or 2 people
9. Clothed
10. Quiet; still; inactive
12. Reprimand; scold
14. Inactive; not working; being lazy
16. Considering thoughtfully
18. Mooed
21. To long for; to have feelings of tenderness for
22. Intent of ill-will
23. Tarried; loitered; also means flirted
24. In a contrary way
25. Gruff

Down
1. Showing moral excellence, virtue, or chastity
3. Highest point
4. Reluctant
6. Cringing in fear
7. In a state of wonder or amazement
8. Unreasonably ill-tempered
10. Grumblingly; complainingly
11. Like a slave
12. Gave reluctantly or resentfully
13. Full of strength and energy
15. Bold and offensive
17. Blurred and/or reddened
19. Twist; squirm; contort
20. Thrifty; tight with money
23. Raised platform

Good Earth Vocabulary Crossword 3 Answer Key

Across
1. Characterized by fluent speech
2. Withered; wrinkled
5. Small, two-wheeled carriage pulled by 1 or 2 people
9. Clothed
10. Quiet; still; inactive
12. Reprimand; scold
14. Inactive; not working; being lazy
16. Considering thoughtfully
18. Mooed
21. To long for; to have feelings of tenderness for
22. Intent of ill-will
23. Tarried; loitered; also means flirted
24. In a contrary way
25. Gruff

Down
1. Showing moral excellence, virtue, or chastity
3. Highest point
4. Reluctant
6. Cringing in fear
7. In a state of wonder or amazement
8. Unreasonably ill-tempered
10. Grumblingly; complainingly
11. Like a slave
12. Gave reluctantly or resentfully
13. Full of strength and energy
15. Bold and offensive
17. Blurred and/or reddened
19. Twist; squirm; contort
20. Thrifty; tight with money
23. Raised platform

Good Earth Vocabulary Crossword 4

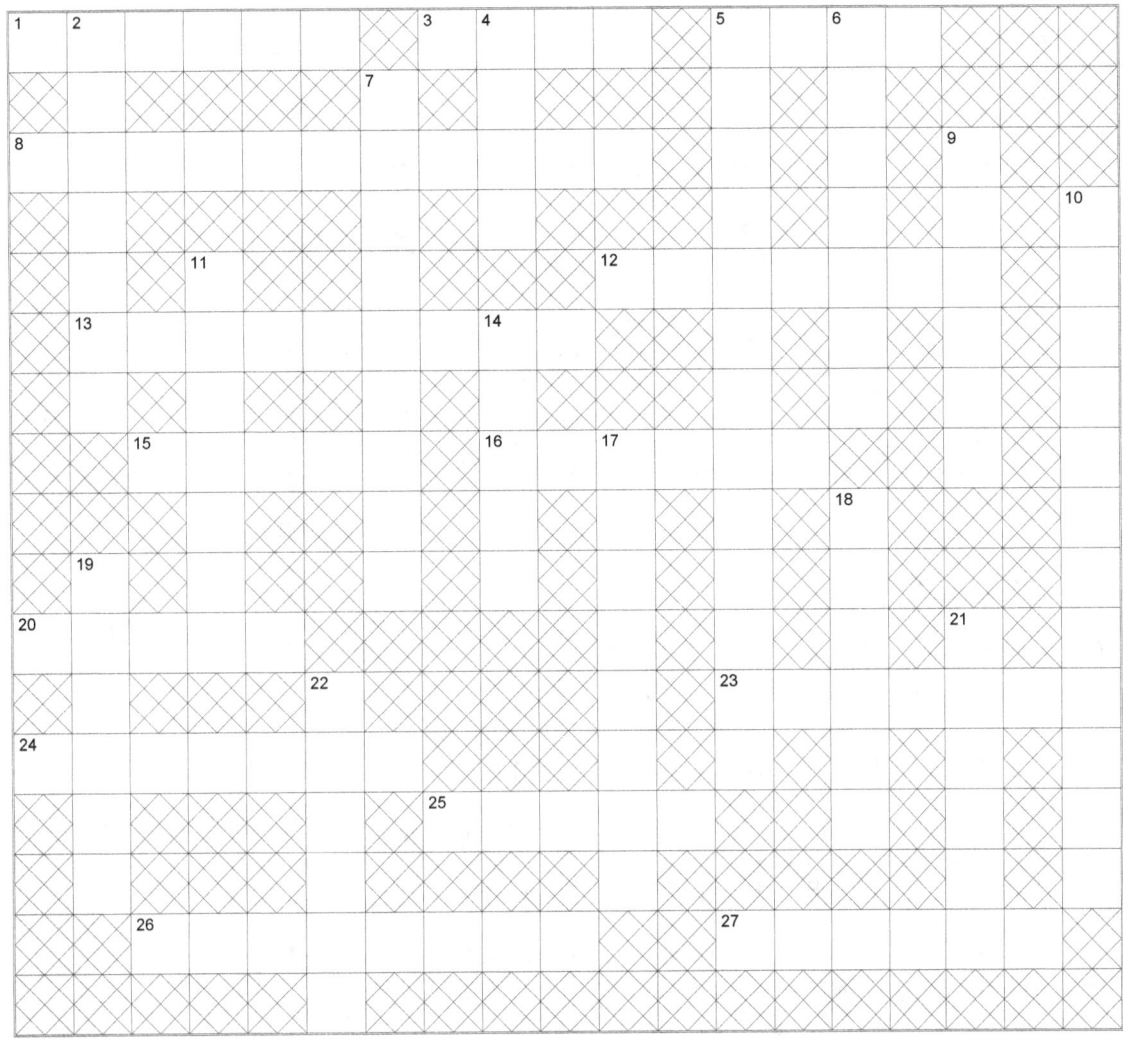

Across
1. Thrifty; tight with money
3. Inactive; not working; being lazy
5. Clothed
8. Persistently pleading
12. Deserving pity
13. Like a slave
15. In a state of wonder or amazement
16. Passionate; full of strong feeling or enthusiasm
20. To long for; to have feelings of tenderness for
23. Having or showing great wealth
24. Withered; wrinkled
25. Mooed
26. Cringing in fear
27. Purified; rid of undesirable elements

Down
2. Bitter regret
4. Raised platform
5. State of paralyzing dismay
6. Difficult
7. Quiet; still; inactive
9. Considering thoughtfully
10. Making less of something
11. Lack of energy; listlessness
14. Reluctant
17. Objected
18. Full of strength and energy
19. Highest point
21. Reprimand; scold
22. Harvested; cut and collected

Good Earth Vocabulary Crossword 4 Answer Key

Across
1. Thrifty; tight with money
3. Inactive; not working; being lazy
5. Clothed
8. Persistently pleading
12. Deserving pity
13. Like a slave
15. In a state of wonder or amazement
16. Passionate; full of strong feeling or enthusiasm
20. To long for; to have feelings of tenderness for
23. Having or showing great wealth
24. Withered; wrinkled
25. Mooed
26. Cringing in fear
27. Purified; rid of undesirable elements

Down
2. Bitter regret
4. Raised platform
5. State of paralyzing dismay
6. Difficult
7. Quiet; still; inactive
9. Considering thoughtfully
10. Making less of something
11. Lack of energy; listlessness
14. Reluctant
17. Objected
18. Full of strength and energy
19. Highest point
21. Reprimand; scold
22. Harvested; cut and collected

Good Earth Vocabulary Juggle Letters 1

1. EINZHT = 1. _____
   Highest point

2. NAEYR = 2. _____
   To long for; to have feelings of tenderness for

3. ORSMERE = 3. _____
   Bitter regret

4. ADIS = 4. _____
   Raised platform

5. DCAL = 5. _____
   Clothed

6. ERTAND = 6. _____
   Passionate; full of strong feeling or enthusiasm

7. VESYHEPLI = 7. _____
   In a contrary way

8. RDEUGP = 8. _____
   Purified; rid of undesirable elements

9. TIEUDNMP = 9. _____
   Bold and offensive

10. RTRLBUBEMEIPA =10. _____
    Unshakable; calm and steady

11. COUSUTNU =11. _____
    Slick; characterized by insincere earnestness

12. DEARPE =12. _____
    Harvested; cut and collected

13. PENLAUTT =13. _____
    Unreasonably ill-tempered

14. DRMEDRUE =14. _____
    Objected

15. UEYLOSULRUQ =15. _____
    Grumblingly; complainingly

Good Earth Vocabulary Juggle Letters 1 Answer Key

1. EINZHT = 1. ZENITH
   Highest point
2. NAEYR = 2. YEARN
   To long for; to have feelings of tenderness for
3. ORSMERE = 3. REMORSE
   Bitter regret
4. ADIS = 4. DAIS
   Raised platform
5. DCAL = 5. CLAD
   Clothed
6. ERTAND = 6. ARDENT
   Passionate; full of strong feeling or enthusiasm
7. VESYHEPLI = 7. PEEVISHLY
   In a contrary way
8. RDEUGP = 8. PURGED
   Purified; rid of undesirable elements
9. TIEUDNMP = 9. IMPUDENT
   Bold and offensive
10. RTRLBUBEMEIPA = 10. IMPERTURBABLE
    Unshakable; calm and steady
11. COUSUTNU = 11. UNCTUOUS
    Slick; characterized by insincere earnestness
12. DEARPE = 12. REAPED
    Harvested; cut and collected
13. PENLAUTT = 13. PETULANT
    Unreasonably ill-tempered
14. DRMEDRUE = 14. DEMURRED
    Objected
15. UEYLOSULRUQ = 15. QUERULOUSLY
    Grumblingly; complainingly

Good Earth Vocabulary Juggle Letters 2

1. LBUVOYL = 1. _____
   Characterized by fluent speech

2. OARDUUS = 2. _____
   Difficult

3. EPRGDU = 3. _____
   Purified; rid of undesirable elements

4. OYRTQEUC = 4. _____
   Flirting

5. GURHTTDISA = 5. _____
   Emotionally upset

6. ARLBTEMPIUBRE = 6. _____
   Unshakable; calm and steady

7. TPATLENU = 7. _____
   Unreasonably ill-tempered

8. EGEGBRUDD = 8. _____
   Gave reluctantly or resentfully

9. HATOL = 9. _____
   Reluctant

10. DAGPOA =10. _____
    Multi-story Buddhist tower

11. APAGE =11. _____
    In a state of wonder or amazement

12. ONTIMUNPRGI =12. _____
    Persistently pleading

13. SANSICETN =13. _____
    Continuous

14. ITATCNNSONERO =14. _____
    State of paralyzing dismay

15. ALDC =15. _____
    Clothed

Good Earth Vocabulary Juggle Letters 2 Answer Key

1. LBUVOYL = 1. VOLUBLY
   Characterized by fluent speech

2. OARDUUS = 2. ARDUOUS
   Difficult

3. EPRGDU = 3. PURGED
   Purified; rid of undesirable elements

4. OYRTQEUC = 4. COQUETRY
   Flirting

5. GURHTTDISA = 5. DISTRAUGHT
   Emotionally upset

6. ARLBTEMPIUBRE = 6. IMPERTURBABLE
   Unshakable; calm and steady

7. TPATLENU = 7. PETULANT
   Unreasonably ill-tempered

8. EGEGBRUDD = 8. BEGRUDGED
   Gave reluctantly or resentfully

9. HATOL = 9. LOATH
   Reluctant

10. DAGPOA =10. PAGODA
    Multi-story Buddhist tower

11. APAGE =11. AGAPE
    In a state of wonder or amazement

12. ONTIMUNPRGI =12. IMPORTUNING
    Persistently pleading

13. SANSICETN =13. INCESSANT
    Continuous

14. ITATCNNSONERO =14. CONSTERNATION
    State of paralyzing dismay

15. ALDC =15. CLAD
    Clothed

Good Earth Vocabulary Juggle Letters 3

1. LERYAB = 1. _____
   Blurred and/or reddened

2. URTYCEOQ = 2. _____
   Flirting

3. TOUCUNSU = 3. _____
   Slick; characterized by insincere earnestness

4. OSNETINANTORC = 4. _____
   State of paralyzing dismay

5. UCQETSINE = 5. _____
   Quiet; still; inactive

6. EGWCNIRO = 6. _____
   Cringing in fear

7. PIERNE = 7. _____
   To be discontented or low in spirits

8. CEIMNEEN = 8. _____
   Position of superiority

9. SORDAUU = 9. _____
   Difficult

10. ECEAICNQUST =10. _____
    Passively agreeable

11. CIRHASK =11. _____
    Small, two-wheeled carriage pulled by 1 or 2 people

12. UEPLNATT =12. _____
    Unreasonably ill-tempered

13. PIEINEATCDOR =13. _____
    Making less of something

14. MBBIUETRPELAR =14. _____
    Unshakable; calm and steady

15. IADS =15. _____
    Raised platform

Good Earth Vocabulary Juggle Letters 3 Answer Key

1. LERYAB = 1. BLEARY
   Blurred and/or reddened

2. URTYCEOQ = 2. COQUETRY
   Flirting

3. TOUCUNSU = 3. UNCTUOUS
   Slick; characterized by insincere earnestness

4. OSNETINANTORC = 4. CONSTERNATION
   State of paralyzing dismay

5. UCQETSINE = 5. QUIESCENT
   Quiet; still; inactive

6. EGWCNIRO = 6. COWERING
   Cringing in fear

7. PIERNE = 7. REPINE
   To be discontented or low in spirits

8. CEIMNEEN = 8. EMINENCE
   Position of superiority

9. SORDAUU = 9. ARDUOUS
   Difficult

10. ECEAICNQUST = 10. ACQUIESCENT
    Passively agreeable

11. CIRHASK = 11. RICKSHA
    Small, two-wheeled carriage pulled by 1 or 2 people

12. UEPLNATT = 12. PETULANT
    Unreasonably ill-tempered

13. PIEINEATCDOR = 13. DEPRECIATION
    Making less of something

14. MBBIUETRPELAR = 14. IMPERTURBABLE
    Unshakable; calm and steady

15. IADS = 15. DAIS
    Raised platform

Good Earth Vocabulary Juggle Letters 4

1. UYIURTSOVL = 1. _____
   Showing moral excellence, virtue, or chastity

2. CATQUNECSEI = 2. _____
   Passively agreeable

3. LILHSVSYA = 3. _____
   Like a slave

4. RBILBETMREPAU = 4. _____
   Unshakable; calm and steady

5. EZNEDWI = 5. _____
   Withered; wrinkled

6. DEOWL = 6. _____
   Mooed

7. EIUETSQNC = 7. _____
   Quiet; still; inactive

8. EPUGDR = 8. _____
   Purified; rid of undesirable elements

9. RUIGTASDTH = 9. _____
   Emotionally upset

10. ULVYOBL = 10. _____
    Characterized by fluent speech

11. ELCMAI = 11. _____
    Intent of ill-will

12. DLECMPELO = 12. _____
    Forced

13. UENMITDP = 13. _____
    Bold and offensive

14. IASD = 14. _____
    Raised platform

15. NMGSIU = 15. _____
    Considering thoughtfully

Good Earth Vocabulary Juggle Letters 4 Answer Key

1. UYIURTSOVL = 1. VIRTUOUSLY
   Showing moral excellence, virtue, or chastity

2. CATQUNECSEI = 2. ACQUIESCENT
   Passively agreeable

3. LILHSVSYA = 3. SLAVISHLY
   Like a slave

4. RBILBETMREPAU = 4. IMPERTURBABLE
   Unshakable; calm and steady

5. EZNEDWI = 5. WIZENED
   Withered; wrinkled

6. DEOWL = 6. LOWED
   Mooed

7. EIUETSQNC = 7. QUIESCENT
   Quiet; still; inactive

8. EPUGDR = 8. PURGED
   Purified; rid of undesirable elements

9. RUIGTASDTH = 9. DISTRAUGHT
   Emotionally upset

10. ULVYOBL = 10. VOLUBLY
    Characterized by fluent speech

11. ELCMAI = 11. MALICE
    Intent of ill-will

12. DLECMPELO = 12. COMPELLED
    Forced

13. UENMITDP = 13. IMPUDENT
    Bold and offensive

14. IASD = 14. DAIS
    Raised platform

15. NMGSIU = 15. MUSING
    Considering thoughtfully

ACQUIESCENT	Passively agreeable
AGAPE	In a state of wonder or amazement
ARDENT	Passionate; full of strong feeling or enthusiasm
ARDUOUS	Difficult
BEGRUDGED	Gave reluctantly or resentfully
BERATE	Reprimand; scold

BLEARY	Blurred and/or reddened
BOISTEROUSLY	Loudly; without restraint
CLAD	Clothed
COMPELLED	Forced
CONCUBINES	Women contracted as second wives
CONSTERNATION	State of paralyzing dismay

CONTRIVED	Devised; planned; managed
COQUETRY	Flirting
COWERING	Cringing in fear
DAIS	Raised platform
DALLIED	Tarried; loitered; also means flirted
DEMURRED	Objected

DEPRECIATION	Making less of something
DISTRAUGHT	Emotionally upset
EMINENCE	Position of superiority
FRUGAL	Thrifty; tight with money
IDLE	Inactive; not working; being lazy
IMPERTURBABLE	Unshakable; calm and steady

IMPORTUNING	Persistently pleading
IMPUDENT	Bold and offensive
INCESSANT	Continuous
LANGUOR	Lack of energy; listlessness
LOATH	Reluctant
LOWED	Mooed

MALICE	Intent of ill-will
MUSING	Considering thoughtfully
OBEISANCES	Gestures of homage, deference, or reverence
OPULENT	Having or showing great wealth
PAGODA	Multi-story Buddhist tower
PEEVISHLY	In a contrary way

PETULANT	Unreasonably ill-tempered
PITEOUS	Deserving pity
PURGED	Purified; rid of undesirable elements
QUERULOUSLY	Grumblingly; complainingly
QUIESCENT	Quiet; still; inactive
REAPED	Harvested; cut and collected

REMORSE	Bitter regret
REPINE	To be discontented or low in spirits
RICKSHA	Small, two-wheeled carriage pulled by 1 or 2 people
ROBUST	Full of strength and energy
SCRUPULOUS	Conscientious; exact
SHREWISH	Ill-humored

SLAVISHLY	Like a slave
SUPPED	Ate
SURLY	Gruff
UNCTUOUS	Slick; characterized by insincere earnestness
VIRTUOUSLY	Showing moral excellence, virtue, or chastity
VOLUBLY	Characterized by fluent speech

WIZENED	Withered; wrinkled
WRITHE	Twist; squirm; contort
YEARN	To long for; to have feelings of tenderness for
ZENITH	Highest point

Good Earth Vocabulary

SURLY	DISTRAUGHT	ARDENT	IMPORTUNING	SCRUPULOUS
IDLE	WIZENED	COQUETRY	MUSING	BLEARY
INCESSANT	PEEVISHLY	FREE SPACE	DEMURRED	LOWED
REPINE	CONCUBINES	QUIESCENT	QUERULOUSLY	PETULANT
FRUGAL	VOLUBLY	AGAPE	DAIS	YEARN

Good Earth Vocabulary

PAGODA	SLAVISHLY	BOISTEROUSLY	OPULENT	BERATE
VIRTUOUSLY	DEPRECIATION	WRITHE	BEGRUDGED	CONTRIVED
SHREWISH	PITEOUS	FREE SPACE	RICKSHA	LANGUOR
MALICE	PURGED	UNCTUOUS	CLAD	CONSTERNATION
ARDUOUS	OBEISANCES	ZENITH	LOATH	IMPUDENT

Good Earth Vocabulary

PURGED	DALLIED	ZENITH	PITEOUS	DEMURRED
CONSTERNATION	SHREWISH	MALICE	REAPED	PETULANT
PAGODA	DAIS	FREE SPACE	IMPUDENT	SURLY
REPINE	QUERULOUSLY	INCESSANT	VOLUBLY	SLAVISHLY
CLAD	LOWED	CONCUBINES	BEGRUDGED	CONTRIVED

Good Earth Vocabulary

WIZENED	DEPRECIATION	LANGUOR	WRITHE	REMORSE
IDLE	AGAPE	LOATH	OPULENT	IMPERTURBABLE
QUIESCENT	FRUGAL	FREE SPACE	DISTRAUGHT	PEEVISHLY
SUPPED	VIRTUOUSLY	ACQUIESCENT	EMINENCE	MUSING
UNCTUOUS	RICKSHA	IMPORTUNING	BOISTEROUSLY	OBEISANCES

Good Earth Vocabulary

REAPED	VIRTUOUSLY	COWERING	PITEOUS	SLAVISHLY
BLEARY	DISTRAUGHT	PAGODA	AGAPE	ARDUOUS
BEGRUDGED	REMORSE	FREE SPACE	SCRUPULOUS	YEARN
IMPUDENT	PEEVISHLY	EMINENCE	OPULENT	QUERULOUSLY
ROBUST	OBEISANCES	COQUETRY	DEPRECIATION	LOATH

Good Earth Vocabulary

CONTRIVED	MUSING	FRUGAL	SHREWISH	REPINE
WIZENED	IDLE	SURLY	BERATE	IMPERTURBABLE
CONSTERNATION	QUIESCENT	FREE SPACE	ZENITH	IMPORTUNING
LANGUOR	VOLUBLY	RICKSHA	INCESSANT	COMPELLED
UNCTUOUS	PETULANT	LOWED	DEMURRED	CONCUBINES

Good Earth Vocabulary

REMORSE	RICKSHA	PITEOUS	PEEVISHLY	INCESSANT
DAIS	EMINENCE	SLAVISHLY	AGAPE	OPULENT
SCRUPULOUS	COQUETRY	FREE SPACE	BERATE	CLAD
LOWED	VOLUBLY	QUIESCENT	SURLY	REPINE
WRITHE	REAPED	YEARN	FRUGAL	PURGED

Good Earth Vocabulary

UNCTUOUS	IMPORTUNING	ARDUOUS	MALICE	IMPUDENT
BEGRUDGED	COWERING	OBEISANCES	DISTRAUGHT	CONCUBINES
BOISTEROUSLY	MUSING	FREE SPACE	DEMURRED	ACQUIESCENT
ZENITH	QUERULOUSLY	ROBUST	IDLE	LOATH
WIZENED	PETULANT	ARDENT	LANGUOR	CONSTERNATION

Good Earth Vocabulary

REAPED	CONTRIVED	LANGUOR	BEGRUDGED	SHREWISH
BOISTEROUSLY	ZENITH	ARDUOUS	EMINENCE	AGAPE
IMPERTURBABLE	UNCTUOUS	FREE SPACE	SLAVISHLY	REPINE
COMPELLED	MUSING	PURGED	QUERULOUSLY	COQUETRY
REMORSE	DEMURRED	CONSTERNATION	DEPRECIATION	LOWED

Good Earth Vocabulary

PITEOUS	BLEARY	INCESSANT	ARDENT	SUPPED
DALLIED	LOATH	VOLUBLY	CLAD	WIZENED
PETULANT	MALICE	FREE SPACE	ROBUST	PEEVISHLY
ACQUIESCENT	VIRTUOUSLY	SCRUPULOUS	PAGODA	IDLE
OPULENT	QUIESCENT	IMPORTUNING	SURLY	COWERING

Good Earth Vocabulary

ACQUIESCENT	PURGED	DEPRECIATION	WRITHE	CONSTERNATION
VIRTUOUSLY	ARDUOUS	COMPELLED	YEARN	SLAVISHLY
WIZENED	PEEVISHLY	FREE SPACE	ROBUST	DISTRAUGHT
SCRUPULOUS	MUSING	REPINE	PETULANT	IDLE
SHREWISH	ARDENT	BEGRUDGED	DAIS	UNCTUOUS

Good Earth Vocabulary

MALICE	REAPED	CLAD	IMPORTUNING	PITEOUS
IMPERTURBABLE	LOATH	CONTRIVED	BERATE	QUIESCENT
IMPUDENT	VOLUBLY	FREE SPACE	ZENITH	LOWED
DALLIED	AGAPE	COWERING	BOISTEROUSLY	SURLY
INCESSANT	OBEISANCES	OPULENT	COQUETRY	QUERULOUSLY

Good Earth Vocabulary

ROBUST	BERATE	DALLIED	VIRTUOUSLY	OPULENT
BEGRUDGED	SLAVISHLY	ZENITH	RICKSHA	IMPORTUNING
COQUETRY	DAIS	FREE SPACE	CONCUBINES	EMINENCE
COMPELLED	ACQUIESCENT	UNCTUOUS	REAPED	OBEISANCES
MUSING	IMPUDENT	BOISTEROUSLY	INCESSANT	QUERULOUSLY

Good Earth Vocabulary

ARDENT	REMORSE	DEMURRED	PURGED	WIZENED
MALICE	REPINE	LOWED	IDLE	YEARN
PEEVISHLY	CONSTERNATION	FREE SPACE	PAGODA	AGAPE
COWERING	SHREWISH	LANGUOR	DISTRAUGHT	SCRUPULOUS
PETULANT	DEPRECIATION	VOLUBLY	CLAD	WRITHE

Good Earth Vocabulary

IMPERTURBABLE	OPULENT	ARDUOUS	MUSING	IDLE
AGAPE	OBEISANCES	BERATE	REPINE	PAGODA
DEMURRED	LOATH	FREE SPACE	WIZENED	PURGED
CONTRIVED	SCRUPULOUS	LOWED	CLAD	FRUGAL
REAPED	COQUETRY	SHREWISH	WRITHE	BLEARY

Good Earth Vocabulary

COMPELLED	QUERULOUSLY	CONSTERNATION	DEPRECIATION	EMINENCE
SUPPED	REMORSE	DISTRAUGHT	UNCTUOUS	DALLIED
QUIESCENT	CONCUBINES	FREE SPACE	INCESSANT	SLAVISHLY
YEARN	LANGUOR	MALICE	ZENITH	VIRTUOUSLY
IMPORTUNING	BOISTEROUSLY	SURLY	BEGRUDGED	RICKSHA

Good Earth Vocabulary

BERATE	OBEISANCES	MUSING	RICKSHA	DEPRECIATION
QUIESCENT	LANGUOR	ROBUST	DALLIED	DAIS
VIRTUOUSLY	INCESSANT	FREE SPACE	IDLE	REAPED
IMPERTURBABLE	REMORSE	REPINE	ARDUOUS	SHREWISH
ACQUIESCENT	PETULANT	IMPORTUNING	WRITHE	COMPELLED

Good Earth Vocabulary

MALICE	CONCUBINES	COWERING	SLAVISHLY	LOWED
SCRUPULOUS	ARDENT	PITEOUS	SUPPED	IMPUDENT
BEGRUDGED	UNCTUOUS	FREE SPACE	LOATH	COQUETRY
CONSTERNATION	WIZENED	AGAPE	DISTRAUGHT	PAGODA
CONTRIVED	VOLUBLY	BLEARY	FRUGAL	CLAD

Good Earth Vocabulary

SHREWISH	QUIESCENT	ACQUIESCENT	ZENITH	PEEVISHLY
PETULANT	WIZENED	PURGED	SUPPED	OPULENT
SCRUPULOUS	VOLUBLY	FREE SPACE	UNCTUOUS	COQUETRY
AGAPE	SURLY	REMORSE	BERATE	ARDENT
PAGODA	MALICE	BEGRUDGED	FRUGAL	DAIS

Good Earth Vocabulary

CONTRIVED	IMPERTURBABLE	MUSING	BOISTEROUSLY	PITEOUS
OBEISANCES	LOATH	LANGUOR	CONCUBINES	IMPORTUNING
INCESSANT	SLAVISHLY	FREE SPACE	QUERULOUSLY	BLEARY
DALLIED	CLAD	REPINE	LOWED	CONSTERNATION
ROBUST	VIRTUOUSLY	REAPED	RICKSHA	EMINENCE

Good Earth Vocabulary

REMORSE	BOISTEROUSLY	EMINENCE	VOLUBLY	ARDENT
LOATH	IMPORTUNING	SCRUPULOUS	QUERULOUSLY	BEGRUDGED
IMPUDENT	BERATE	FREE SPACE	DEMURRED	OBEISANCES
IMPERTURBABLE	IDLE	ZENITH	QUIESCENT	ROBUST
FRUGAL	DISTRAUGHT	AGAPE	UNCTUOUS	INCESSANT

Good Earth Vocabulary

CONCUBINES	COWERING	WIZENED	REPINE	COQUETRY
LOWED	WRITHE	VIRTUOUSLY	COMPELLED	CONSTERNATION
CONTRIVED	RICKSHA	FREE SPACE	MUSING	SURLY
PETULANT	DALLIED	BLEARY	DEPRECIATION	ACQUIESCENT
ARDUOUS	PAGODA	CLAD	OPULENT	DAIS

Good Earth Vocabulary

AGAPE	DISTRAUGHT	LANGUOR	BOISTEROUSLY	DALLIED
SLAVISHLY	REPINE	QUIESCENT	WIZENED	PEEVISHLY
SCRUPULOUS	MALICE	FREE SPACE	DAIS	SUPPED
RICKSHA	FRUGAL	UNCTUOUS	DEMURRED	COMPELLED
LOATH	ARDENT	OBEISANCES	COWERING	IDLE

Good Earth Vocabulary

VIRTUOUSLY	PAGODA	REMORSE	BLEARY	INCESSANT
CLAD	BERATE	PURGED	ROBUST	WRITHE
CONCUBINES	BEGRUDGED	FREE SPACE	ACQUIESCENT	PITEOUS
MUSING	COQUETRY	IMPUDENT	CONSTERNATION	ZENITH
IMPERTURBABLE	SHREWISH	QUERULOUSLY	PETULANT	VOLUBLY

Good Earth Vocabulary

COWERING	ZENITH	AGAPE	CONSTERNATION	LANGUOR
ARDUOUS	PURGED	MUSING	IMPUDENT	BEGRUDGED
REAPED	ROBUST	FREE SPACE	EMINENCE	SLAVISHLY
ACQUIESCENT	QUERULOUSLY	INCESSANT	DEPRECIATION	OPULENT
IMPERTURBABLE	DALLIED	CONCUBINES	IMPORTUNING	DEMURRED

Good Earth Vocabulary

WRITHE	DAIS	COQUETRY	LOATH	CLAD
VIRTUOUSLY	BERATE	SCRUPULOUS	MALICE	UNCTUOUS
SHREWISH	QUIESCENT	FREE SPACE	BLEARY	PAGODA
IDLE	REMORSE	PITEOUS	LOWED	VOLUBLY
CONTRIVED	FRUGAL	PETULANT	ARDENT	RICKSHA

Good Earth Vocabulary

QUERULOUSLY	CONTRIVED	CLAD	OBEISANCES	RICKSHA
YEARN	BERATE	PURGED	DEMURRED	SHREWISH
MUSING	ARDUOUS	FREE SPACE	ROBUST	DAIS
LOATH	DISTRAUGHT	INCESSANT	ZENITH	BOISTEROUSLY
SLAVISHLY	WIZENED	PITEOUS	LOWED	VOLUBLY

Good Earth Vocabulary

COWERING	BLEARY	IMPUDENT	DALLIED	SCRUPULOUS
COMPELLED	WRITHE	ACQUIESCENT	PEEVISHLY	COQUETRY
OPULENT	REMORSE	FREE SPACE	SUPPED	IMPORTUNING
REPINE	UNCTUOUS	VIRTUOUSLY	ARDENT	DEPRECIATION
IDLE	SURLY	REAPED	PAGODA	EMINENCE

Good Earth Vocabulary

DEMURRED	ROBUST	SUPPED	ARDUOUS	PITEOUS
COWERING	PEEVISHLY	ACQUIESCENT	PURGED	QUIESCENT
DEPRECIATION	CONCUBINES	FREE SPACE	COQUETRY	FRUGAL
EMINENCE	OBEISANCES	BLEARY	LOATH	REMORSE
IMPUDENT	SHREWISH	YEARN	INCESSANT	DAIS

Good Earth Vocabulary

SLAVISHLY	BOISTEROUSLY	DISTRAUGHT	ZENITH	DALLIED
MUSING	IMPORTUNING	SCRUPULOUS	QUERULOUSLY	COMPELLED
VIRTUOUSLY	BEGRUDGED	FREE SPACE	BERATE	AGAPE
PAGODA	WIZENED	LANGUOR	CONTRIVED	MALICE
CLAD	LOWED	PETULANT	UNCTUOUS	RICKSHA

Good Earth Vocabulary

UNCTUOUS	LANGUOR	BERATE	COQUETRY	ARDUOUS
SHREWISH	PURGED	SUPPED	MUSING	DAIS
VOLUBLY	BEGRUDGED	FREE SPACE	DALLIED	INCESSANT
CONCUBINES	REMORSE	CLAD	ARDENT	PAGODA
ROBUST	AGAPE	IMPUDENT	IMPORTUNING	DEMURRED

Good Earth Vocabulary

WRITHE	EMINENCE	SCRUPULOUS	ZENITH	QUIESCENT
LOWED	SLAVISHLY	MALICE	QUERULOUSLY	REAPED
FRUGAL	DISTRAUGHT	FREE SPACE	OBEISANCES	VIRTUOUSLY
ACQUIESCENT	WIZENED	BOISTEROUSLY	COWERING	OPULENT
BLEARY	PEEVISHLY	CONSTERNATION	PETULANT	COMPELLED

www.ingramcontent.com/pod-product-compliance
Lightning Source LLC
Chambersburg PA
CBHW081455070526
44586CB00019B/2360